THE ISRAELI-PALESTINIAN CONFLICT

UNDERSTANDING THE FORCES THAT DRIVE DIVISION

CONRAD PRESLEY

For permissions requests, speaking inquiries, and bulk order purchase options, email: publishing@uconcept.com.

ISBN: 978-1-960188-23-6 | E-book

ISBN: 978-1-960188-22-9 | Paperback

ISBN: 978-1-960188-21-2 | Hardcover

Published by Unlimited Concepts, Coconut Creek, Florida.

www.publishing.uconcept.com

Book, Editing, and Cover Design by Janet Garcia | UConceptDesigns.com

Published in the United States of America.

To my brother...

Who's always enjoyed a good reading and likes to engage in interesting debates. May you enjoy this book as much as I enjoyed writing it.

CONTENTS

Introduction   13

1. THE SEEDS OF STRIFE: TRACING THE
   HISTORICAL ROOTS   19
   The Early Jewish and Arab Societies   19
   World War I and the Balfour Declaration   25

2. THE CHESSBOARD OF CONFLICT - KEY PLAYERS
   AND THEIR MOVES   35
   Power from Within: Fatah, Hamas, and the
   Israeli Government   35
   Fatah: Movement for the National Liberation of
   Palestine   36
   Hamas: Islamic Resistance Movement   38
   The Israeli Government's Role in the Israeli-
   Palestinian Conflict   40
   The United States Role in the Israeli-Palestinian
   Conflict   42
   The United Nations' Role in the Israeli-
   Palestinian Conflict   44
   The European Union's Role in the Israeli-
   Palestinian Conflict   46
   The Arab League's Role in the Israeli-Palestinian
   Conflict   47
   The Role of Other Middle Eastern States in the
   Israeli-Palestinian Conflict   49
   The Role of Non-Governmental Organizations
   (NGOs)   51
   The Role of Civil Society in the Conflict   54
   The Role of Public Opinion   56

3. THE DOMINO EFFECT: UNDERSTANDING THE
   SOCIO-ECONOMIC IMPACT OF THE CONFLICT   59
   The Weight of War: Economic Struggles Faced
   by Israelis and Palestinians   60
   Health and Conflict: The Struggle for Well-being   66
   Everyday Life Amid Conflict: The Struggle for
   Normalcy   69
   Looking Forward: The Socio-Economic Future
   Amid Conflict   72

4. THE POLITICAL CHESSBOARD:
   UNDERSTANDING THE ISRAEL-PALESTINE
   POWER PLAY   77
   Political Ideologies: The Foundations of the
   Conflict   77
   Political Parties: The Key Players   83
   Palestine: A Complex Mosaic   85
   Political Processes: Navigating the Maze   87
   Israel's Political Processes: Elections and
   Coalition Building   87

5. THE CURRENT STATE OF AFFAIRS:
   UNDERSTANDING RECENT DEVELOPMENTS   93
   The Trump Era: A Shift in American Policy   94
   The Abraham Accords: A New Direction for
   Middle East Diplomacy   96
   The Israeli Political Scene: A Period of Instability   99
   The Gaza Conflicts: A Cycle of Violence and its
   Humanitarian Impact   102
   The West Bank: Ongoing Settlement Expansion
   and its Implications   105
   The Palestinian Authority: Political Divisions
   and Challenges   108

6. DECODING THE SOLUTIONS: A PATH TO PEACE   113
   The Two-State Solution: Navigating the Path to
   a Separate Peace   113
   The One-State Solution: Paving the Way to a
   United Future   116

Other Proposed Solutions: Navigating Paths to a
United Future   118
The Role of the International Community:
Facilitating a Solution   131
Examining the Way Forward: An Ongoing
Journey   135

7. CONCLUSION   139

About the Author   147
Bibliography   149

LEAVE A 1-CLICK REVIEW

Customer Reviews

★★★★★ 2
5.0 out of 5 stars ▾

5 star	100%
4 star	0%
3 star	0%
2 star	0%
1 star	0%

See all verified purchase reviews ›

Share your thoughts with other customers

Write a customer review

I would be incredibly thankful if you take just
60-seconds to write a brief review on Amazon,
even if it's just a few sentences!

https://amazon.com/review/create-review?asin=1960188224

INTRODUCTION

The Israeli-Palestinian conflict is an unending issue and it is not going to end anytime soon. But it is not a recent matter, neither is it just a regional tussle. It is a very intricate and long-standing conflict that has been occurring for over a century. This conflict, from inception, has been a source of suffering, loss of lives, cause of political tension, and a cause for concern globally.

The conflict is an intertwining of various events, players, and powers. At the heart of it lies the struggle for sovereignty, superiority, religion, and claims to blurred territories. These various forces have led to hostility and division among the two major players - Israel and Palestine, and are undeniably one of the most longstanding and profound conflicts of all time. As of the time of this writing, people are still getting killed and displaced, and the fires of war continue to rage on in this region.

The roots of this conflict go way back in history. It represents a story of two communities with ancient claims and contemporary ambitions. The conflict is ignited and fueled by different historical events that have deeply scarred the major players in their way. So, if we want to understand this conflict and find a way forward, in that case, we must start by delving into the history and unearthing the events that have led to this present point.

One of these historical events is the Zionist movement of the 19th century. This Jewish nationalist movement consisted of a group of individuals who aimed to establish a Jewish homeland in Palestine, which led to a series of ripple events like the Balfour Declaration of 1917 issued by the British government. This declaration gave the Zionists what they clamored for while also promising to protect the interest of the Arabs. However, this Balfour Declaration, while welcomed by one party - the Jews in Palestine, was unsatisfactory for the Arabs who felt marginalized in their land, and that set the stage for the ongoing strife and struggle for territorial dominance.

While there are two major players in this conflict - the Jews, who wanted self-determination and a homeland in this region, and the Palestinians, who also wanted self-governance and control of ancestral lands - there are other forces that are equally catalysts of a crisis that will last for over a decade.

One such player was Arthur Balfour, who issued the Balfour Declaration to set the conflict in motion. Also, the British Mandate administration created mandatory Palestine and governed the region after World War 1, and the United Nations in 1947 when passed the partition plan that proposed the creation of separate states for the Jews and Arabs. However, this proposal by the United Nations was met with resistance and ultimately culminated in a war that led to the establishment of Israel, a sovereign state for the Jews.

The regional dynamics of this conflict are another significant force behind the conflict as neighboring countries like Egypt, Syria, and Jordan became entwined in many conflicts, adding layers to the already complex situation. Israel came out of the independence war with a larger territory than recognized by the other parties in the war, and this led to another outburst by the Palestinians, who were not satisfied with the outcome and couldn't agree with it. The territories, which include the West Bank, Gaza Strip, and East Jerusalem, each holding historical and strategic significance, were considered sacred by multiple faiths and thereby caused further tensions when they were conquered and made part of the new state of Israel in the 1967 Six-Day war.

Another major player in the Israeli-Palestinian conflict is religion. Jerusalem is a city that holds sacred values for Christians, Jews, and Muslims who have lived there for many years. Monuments like the Church of the Holy Sepulcher the Western Wall, and the Al-Aqsa Mosque, which belong to each of these religions, were all located within a small area of the City, and that greatly magnified the intensity of the conflict. Moreso, when Israel tried to lay claim to a city that holds memories and values for the Jews and Arabs alike. The Palestinians just couldn't agree to this claim, and this religious connection to

Jerusalem by the two parties made it hard for them to reach a consensus.

As the conflict has persisted over the years, there have been many efforts at resolution. From the Oslo Accords of the 1990s to the Camp David Summit in 2000 and the more recent Annapolis conference of 2007, various diplomatic steps and efforts have been poured towards resolving this longstanding conflict.

The two-state solution is another attempt at a resolution that remains widely discussed to date. It is a solution that attempts to create a coexistence of Israel and a future Palestinian state. However, this attempt has struggled to find real implementation as the status of Jerusalem and its borders and the right of return for Palestinian refugees remain points of contention during negotiations. Every attempt at resolution has presented a different and unique set of challenges that kept the conflict rolling to this day.

While this conflict is nationalized in the Israeli-Palestinian regions, the effect is not confined to the region. Instead, the ripple effect is felt on a global scale as it actively impacts geopolitics, security, and peace. The search for a conflict resolution for these two parties holds significant implications for diplomatic and international relations.

For example, the quest for peace has influenced Israel's interactions and relations with neighboring countries, especially Egypt and Jordan. Also, the United States' role as a mediator and the regional influence of countries like Iran and Turkey shapes the geopolitical landscape.

This longstanding conflict profoundly affects global security concerns due to the potential for escalation and has proven to be beyond a geopolitical struggle. It is a test of the moral and ethical principles of humanity. It is a test for the commitment to human rights, peace, and self-determination, and the resolution of the conflict is a potentially powerful statement for international morality. Hence, various players are involved to ensure a lasting solution.

The conflict between these two parties is an intricate culmination of historical events, territorial disputes, religion, and the goals and aspirations of two groups of people. Understanding the complexity of this conflict will not only foster peace but will also promote empathy for the parties involved.

As we flip through the pages of histories and the intertwined web of forces that have led to the division between these two players, we will begin to get a deeper comprehension of the conflict that has held these two nations for over a decade and the possible challenges that lie ahead. Understanding the history, religious and cultural ties, and global consequences will help us grasp the true essence of the Israeli-Palestinian conflict. This informed understanding is what this book aims to accomplish. Chapter after Chapter, we will peel off different layers of what made the Palestinian-Israeli conflict what it is today. We will look at the history of the Jews and Arabs and how they lived independently and co-dependently in the past. We will also examine the individuals and groups who have actively or passively had an influence on this conflict from the past up to the present day.

The first Chapter will look at the history of these two main characters, and subsequent chapters will further explore other players in the conflict and how they've contributed to this war that has turned into a global phenomenon. At the end of the book, we hope to have gotten an unbiased opinion of what exactly led to the conflict and possible paths to peace and conflict resolution.

THE SEEDS OF STRIFE: TRACING THE HISTORICAL ROOTS

The first thing we need to do to understand the conflict is go deep into these two sides' history. We must dig into the backstory and determine where this drama comes from. It's like a long, complicated story with two main characters – Israel and Palestine – and it's been going on for over a hundred years. So, let's break it down.

THE EARLY JEWISH AND ARAB SOCIETIES

- **The Jewish Society**

The early Jewish society, with its history spanning a millennium, begins from the ancient times in the biblical documentation up until the era of the second temple. This society's journey through time is full of significant historical phases, events, and geographic regions. We can trace the roots of the

Jews to the ancient Israelites recorded in the Bible. They are a Semitic people currently found in present-days: Israel and Palestine. According to biblical narratives, the Jews were a descendant of the twelve sons of Jacob - later known as Israel, which remains the name of the society to date.

Early Jewish society was characterized by their monotheistic religious belief in Yahweh or Jehovah - The God of Israel. Their religious and moral teachings were recorded in the Tanakh (or Hebrew Bible) - from where the current modern-day Holy Bible was derived. This sacred text was essential in how the Jews lived their lives as they followed the tenets written therein. They often offered sacrifices to Yahweh at the Jerusalem temple, observed the Sabbath day, and celebrated festivals like the Passover Feast, Yom Kippur, and Sukkot.

All through their history, Jewish communities underwent periods of dispersion and exile in foreign lands. One such was the Babylonian Exile, which lasted from 586 to 539 BCE. After this particular dispersion, Jewish communities began to cluster in different regions, leading to a Jewish diaspora. These diaspora communities were present in places such as Rome, Alexandria, and Babylonia, and they became vital centers of Jewish life.

The second temple period (516 BCE to 70 CE) marked a crucial phase in Jewish history as it was during this time that the second temple was reconstructed, and Judaism as a religion or way of life underwent significant transformations. It was at this time that different sects like the Pharisees, the Sadducees and the Essenes submerged marking a major shift in the religious landscape of the Jews.

This second Temple period was established during the Roman rule. At the time, tensions between the Jewish population and the Roman authorities escalated and led to the Jewish-Roman wars, which ultimately led to the destruction of the second temple in 70 CE.

The destruction of this temple was a major milestone and defining moment in the history of the Jews. They endured various trials and tribulations and were able to preserve their culture and religion, leading to the post-destruction era.

- **Early Arab Society**

Similar to the Early Jewish society, the Early Arab society also had a captivating and interesting history. The Early Arabs were mainly found in the Arabian peninsula, significantly influencing the region's development.

Prior to the 7th century and the advent of the Islamic religion, the Arabian society was divided into different tribes and clans. The region's harsh and arid environment led most Early Arabs to a nomadic lifestyle involving herding and trading.

Unlike the Early Jewish society, which was monotheistic, the Pre-Islamic Early Arab society was a Polytheist society, and different tribes worshipped different deities. The Kaaba in Mecca later emerged and became the central religious shrine and attracted pilgrims from various Arabian tribes, leading to the growth of Islam among the Arabs.

This emergence of Islam in the 7th century marked a significant milestone and transformative time in the history of the early Arabs. At this time, Prophet Mohammed (SWT) received some revelations from Allah (God) and began to preach a monotheistic message. This message proclaimed by the prophet Mohammed led to the spread of the Islamic religion, the unification of the Arabian Peninsula, and the rapid expansion of Arab culture and influence.

After the death of the prophet, the Arabian Caliphates, which included the Rashidun and Umayyad Caliphates, began to expand into neighboring regions like the Middle East, Spain, and North Africa. This expansion promoted the spread of the Arabic language, the culture, and the Islamic civilization as a whole.

Apart from these religious and territorial expansions, the Early Arab society also made contributions to fields like mathematics, medicine, literature, and astronomy through scholars like Ibn Sina (Avicenna) and Al-Razi. These scholars preserved and improved knowledge from ancient civilizations and improved the world's knowledge base.

This Legacy of the Early Arab is often celebrated as the Islamic Golden Stage, as it was at the forefront of preserving and translating classical works of the Greeks, Romans, and other ancient cultures into the Arabic language. It also set the stage for subsequent scientific, philosophical, and cultural developments.

Together, these early Jewish and Arab societies are essential to the history and culture of the Middle East. They played pivotal roles in shaping the world's religious, cultural, and intellectual landscapes, leaving indelible imprints on future generations. Within these separate societies, there are also people known as Arab Jews.

- **Arab Jews**

While the Early Jews and Arabs were distinct societies, there was a subset of these two societies often referred to as the Arab Jews. The Jews have always been present in Arab society for a long time. These Jewish communities were well-established and often found in the Arabian Peninsula, Mesopotamia, and the Levant long before the advent of Islam in the 7th century and were one of the diverse societies of the region.

Before Islam found its way into Arabian society, Jewish communities thrived in places like Medina and Yathrib, as the Arabian Peninsula housed many tribes with Jews, Christians, and various pagan tribes coexisting. The relationship between Jewish communities and the Arab population is quite complex and marked by alliances and conflicts.

However, the rise of Islam under the leadership of Prophet Muhammad brought about major changes for Arab Jews. With the spread of Islam, the Jews were confronted with new challenges and opportunities, and the Quran recognized Jews as "People of the Book," granting them a protected status and the freedom to practice their religion.

These Arab Jews found an environment within the Islamic Arab that allowed them to preserve their religious and cultural heritage, and they played essential roles as scholars, merchants, and artisans. These Arab Jews contributed significantly to the intellectual and economic life of the Islamic world, as Arabic was the common language for both the Jews and Arabs.

One of the most remarkable periods in the history of these Arab Jews will be the Golden Age (8th to 12th century) of Jewish culture in Spain and the Middle East, which saw them making contributions to various fields like:

1. **Philosophy and Science:** Jewish scholars such as Maimonides (Rambam) made noteworthy contributions to philosophy and science, and his works were highly regarded in both Jewish and Arab circles.
2. **Literature and Poetry:** Arab Jewish poets like Solomon Ibn Gabirol and Judah Halevi crafted beautiful Arabic poetry, drawing from Jewish and Arabic literary traditions.
3. **Interfaith Relations:** Arab Jews frequently engaged in dialogues with Muslim and Christian scholars, fostering cultural exchange and mutual influence.
4. **Trade and Commerce:** Jewish merchants played pivotal roles in the Silk Road trade routes, connecting East and West.

It is noteworthy that despite the success of the Arab Jews, their experiences varied across time and region as they enjoyed relative security at some point and also faced persecution and discrimination at other times.

However, the 20th century brought dramatic changes to the Arab Jews with the rise of Zionism in parenthesis: (a movement for re-establishment of the Jewish nation, known today as Israel) which led to tensions between Arab Jews and the Arab nationalist movement. While some of these people supported the Zionist's idea of a Jewish homeland in the Palestinian region, others were against it. That led to the mass migration of Arab Jews - The Mizrahi Exodus - to Israel in the mid-20th century as a result of rising hostility and violence.

Today, Arab Jews continue to exist in different parts of the world, including Israel, where they have heavily impacted the country's culture and society.

WORLD WAR I AND THE BALFOUR DECLARATION

Named after the issuer, the Balfour Declaration is one of the documents that served as the remote and early causes of Conflict between Israelis and Palestinians. Few documents have had as profound an impact as the Balfour Declaration. This 1917 letter, issued by Arthur Balfour, then British Foreign Secretary, pledged British support for the establishment of a "national home for the Jewish people" in Palestine. From the point it was issued till now, the Balfour Declaration remains a crucial point of interest for the two parties.

More than a decade later, the Balfour Declaration's legacy remains a topic of international discussions and a vital aspect of the quest for the resolution of the Israeli-Palestinian conflict. This declaration from the point of issuance has been a point of contention, and today, the two parties are still at loggerheads, with both suffering heavy casualties like displacement of citizens, waste of economic resources, and the loss of innocent lives.

From Palestine's point of view, the declaration is a historical injustice as they firmly believe that it is responsible for the displacement of the Arabs and the unlawful establishment of the state of Israel. The Palestinian Arabs believed that the declaration greatly violated their rights as the region's indigenous population. On the other hand, Israel sees the declaration as the document that laid the foundation for their independence and recognition as a sovereign nation. They believe that the declaration is a testament to the Jewish historical ties to the land and their right to self-determination.

The Balfour Declaration is such an important document that it still gets referenced in international diplomatic efforts to resolve the conflict between these two nations as it is responsible for creating the delicate issue of who has rights or claims to the land.

Many people tend to ask, "What led to the Balfour Declaration?" and the answer is not necessarily simple. During World War I, the British Government, while looking to gain support from Jewish communities and undermine the influence of the German and Ottoman Empire in the Middle East, sent a letter to Lord Rothschild on November 2, 1917.

Lord Rothschild was a prominent figure in the British Jewish community, and the letter (later known as the Balfour Declaration) sent to him read:

"His Majesty's Government view with favor the establishment in Palestine, of a national home for the Jewish people, and will use their best endeavors to facilitate the achievement of this objective, it being clearly understood that nothing shall be done which may prejudice the civil and religious rights of existing non-Jewish communities in Palestine or the rights and political status enjoyed by Jews in any other country."

As simple as the statement made in the declaration sounds, it catalyzed a series of events that would significantly affect the region. Some of the effects include:

1. **The Empowerment of the Zionist movement:** The Balfour Declaration gave a major boost to the Zionist movement, which had been advocating for the establishment of a Jewish homeland in Palestine. The Zionists saw the declaration as an endorsement of their aspirations, and that led to increased immigration of Jews to Palestine.
2. **Arab Opposition:** Conversely, the declaration was met with opposition by the Palestinian Arabs. They saw this declaration as a betrayal because it was made without their consultation or consent, and this served as the foundation for decades of tension between the Jewish settlers and Arab residents.
3. **British Mandate:** After World War I, The League of Nations granted Great Britain the mandate to administer Palestine. The Balfour Declaration was incorporated into this mandate, and it placed Britain

in the position of having to balance the conflicting interests of Arabs and Jews. We will talk more about the British mandate shortly, as it holds a significant position in the culmination of the conflict between these two parties.

4. **Conflicting Promises:** The Balfour Declaration, although seemingly simple on the surface, contained a caveat - "nothing shall be done which may prejudice the civil and religious rights of existing non-Jewish communities in Palestine - that became the nucleus of many disputes in the years to come.

5. **Post-WWII Immigration:** After the Holocaust, there was an increase in the migration of Jews to Palestine, and this ultimately led to the establishment of the state of Israel in 1948. We cannot deny the influence of the Balfour Declaration on this, as it laid the groundwork for Jewish resettlement in Palestine.

6. **Ongoing Conflict:** The Ongoing Palestinian-Israeli conflict, characterized by wars, peace processes, and ongoing tensions, can trace its roots back to the Balfour Declaration.

Thus, the Balfour Declaration, a century-old document, continues to be at the heart of one of the world's most enduring and deeply rooted conflicts. It is a symbol of the complexity and sensitivity of the Israeli-Palestinian issue, and we cannot overstate its influence on the region.

- **The British Mandate and Its Aftermath**

After World War I had ended, the League of Nations gave Britain the mandate to govern Palestine, leading to the creation of the Mandatory Palestine (with a land mass that covers modern-day Israel, the West Bank, and Gaza). This mandate came into effect in 1920 and was based on the principle of establishing a national home for the Jewish people, as we pointed out earlier. It also promised to protect the civil and religious rights of the non-Jewish communities in Palestine, primarily the Arab population.

During the period of Mandatory Palestine, the Jews received significant support from the British authorities, which led to more Jews coming to the region and the establishment of Jewish institutions in Palestine. Therefore, the Arab population felt marginalized and feared the potential loss of their land and rights and began to revolt. The tensions turned into violent clashes, including the Arab Revolt of 1936-1939, in response to the increasing Jewish immigration. The British government attempted to mediate, but their policies failed to satisfy both parties.

These conflicts continued long into World War II, and by the end of the war, the conflict reached a turning point. The horrors of the Holocaust and the death of six million Jews increased the international support for a Jewish homeland, and in 1947, the United Nations passed a resolution that recommended the partition of the region into separate Jewish and Arab states, with an international regime for Jerusalem.

The Jews welcomed the resolution, but the Arabs vehemently rejected it. This clash of opinion led to the Independence War of 1948. The Mandatory Palestine by the British authority lasted for three decades and significantly impacted the direction of the Israeli-Palestinian conflict, which is still ongoing today.

The joint effect of the Balfour Declaration and the British Mandate remains a point of contention and has resulted in multiple clashes, wars, peace processes, and ongoing tension between Israel, Palestine, and some neighboring nations. The right to Jerusalem, the territorial borders of each nation, the right of return for Palestinian refugees, and the future of Jewish settlements in the West Bank are just a few unresolved issues and serve as a constant threat to peace within the region.

Therefore, it is quite clear that the British Mandate for Palestine played a crucial role in shaping the Israeli-Palestinian conflict. The Balfour Declaration, the conflicting promises to Jewish and Arab communities, and the subsequent events of World War II and the 1948 Arab-Israeli War all contributed to the ongoing strife in the region.

- **The 1948 War and the Establishment of Israel**

The British Mandate ultimately led to the 1948 Independence war. This war, also known as the Arab-Israeli War, led to the establishment of the State of Israel and was a direct consequence of the United Nations' partition plan for Palestine.

In November 1947, the United Nations passed Resolution 181, or the United Nations Partition Plan. This resolution recommended the partition of Mandatory Palestine, which was under

British authority, into two separate states, one for the Jews and one for the Arabs, while Jerusalem would be put under international administration. The Jewish leadership promptly accepted the proposal as it aligned with their goals, but the Arabs rejected it, as they considered it unfair.

Tension brewed from this declaration, and on May 14, 1948, David Ben-Gurion, the head of the Jewish Agency at the time, declared the independence and the establishment of the State of Israel. This declaration came just hours before the expiration of Mandatory Palestine and marked the end of British rule in the region.

Following Israel's declaration of independence, neighboring Arab states, including Egypt, Jordan, Syria, and Iraq, launched a coordinated military intervention in support of the Palestinian Arabs, and this became the start of the 1948 War.

The war saw both sides employing conventional and guerrilla warfare tactics and was characterized by intense fighting and territorial changes. Battles were fought in many locations, including the coastal plain, Negev Desert, and Jerusalem. Both sides experienced gains and losses in these battles, with significant population displacement and suffering on both sides.

Due to its severity, the war led to a series of armistice agreements (often called the Green Line) that were brokered by the United Nations, with the first signed between Israel and Egypt in early 1949, promptly followed by agreements with Jordan, Syria, and Lebanon. These armistice lines established de facto borders, and Israel came out of the war with territorial land that was more than what was allocated to it under the UN Partition Plan.

This war had far-reaching consequences. Israel emerged as an independent state with a significantly altered territorial configuration. The war also displaced hundreds of thousands of Palestinian Arabs, with many becoming refugees.

The Arab-Israeli conflict continued, and the issue of Palestinian refugees and the status of Jerusalem remained unresolved, becoming central points of contention in recent conflicts and peace negotiations. The ongoing Israeli-Palestinian war that has caught global interest is simply a continuation of this conflict and not necessarily a new issue. After the 1948 war, there was another war between these two parties in 1967, dubbed the Six-day War.

- **The Six-Day War in 1967 and Its Repercussions**

A new kind of war broke out after the 1948 war and the declaration of the state of Israel, albeit with a larger territory than intended. Many of the neighboring nations, including Egypt, Jordan, and Syria, were unwilling to accept the post-war Israeli borders. This territorial dispute was creating tension beneath the surface and soon morphed into a volatile situation that was dubbed the Six-Day War of 1967.

One of the immediate triggers for the 1967 war was when Egypt, under the rule of President Gamal Abdel Nasser, closed the Straits of Tiran in May 1967. Israel saw this move as a declaration of war since the straits of Tiran were considered important by Israel as it controlled their access to the port of Eilat.

Responding to this move by Egypt, Israel launched a preemptive strike on June 5, 1967. In this strike, Israel targeted Jordan, Syria, and Egypt. While the war was intense, it only lasted six days, but this was enough to get Israel what it wanted, and the impact was great. This six-day military campaign by Israel was remarkably swift and successful. They gained control of the Sinai Peninsula and the Gaza Strip from Egypt, the West Bank and East Jerusalem from Jordan, and the Golan Heights from Syria. Due to the speed and efficiency of this war, it was called the Six-day War, and the consequence of the war lingers on even today.

The right to Jerusalem was a focal point of the conflict. During the war, Israel reunified Jerusalem, capturing East Jerusalem, which Jordan had held, and after the war, Israel declared Jerusalem as its capital. This move sparked widespread international condemnation and remains a deeply contentious issue.

Another lasting impact of the Six-Day War was Israel's occupation of the West Bank and Gaza Strip. This marked the beginning of an extended Israeli presence in these territories, resulting in complex and enduring conflicts over issues like Israeli settlements and Palestinian self-determination.

The war also further intensified the already strained Israeli-Palestinian relationship as Arab states refused to recognize Israel's right to exist and vowed to regain the captured territories. The Six-Day War heightened Arab nationalism and set the stage for future conflicts in the region.

For the Palestinian people, the war brought displacement and the beginning of the Palestinian refugee issue. It was a crucial moment in the struggle for self-determination by the Palestinians and the foundation of Palestinian nationalism.

In the aftermath of the Six-Day War, the international community took notice. The United Nations Security Council passed Resolution 242, which called for the "withdrawal of Israeli armed forces from territories occupied in the recent conflict" and the "termination of all claims or states of belligerency." This resolution laid the groundwork for diplomatic efforts to find a lasting resolution to the conflict but didn't mark the end of the conflict as the two nations continued to wage war against each other.

THE CHESSBOARD OF CONFLICT - KEY PLAYERS AND THEIR MOVES

With a solid understanding of the history of these two nations engrossed in a longstanding tussle of over a decade, we can begin to see some areas where the problem lies and what possible solutions there could be. However, history doesn't cover it all; it is just a part of the whole. There are many cogs in the wheels of this conflict.

To that end, we'll also explore the players in this conflict, what their contributions were, and how they impacted the conflict.

POWER FROM WITHIN: FATAH, HAMAS, AND THE ISRAELI GOVERNMENT

As we said, many cogs are moving the wheel of the Israeli-Palestinian conflict forward from its inception to date. Some of them from within and some external. From the internal side, we have organizations like Fatah, Hamas, and the Israeli government itself. We'll look at each of these players in as much detail as we can to have a more solid understanding of the crisis. The first player we will examine is the Fatah organization.

FATAH: MOVEMENT FOR THE NATIONAL LIBERATION OF PALESTINE

The Movement for the National Liberation of Palestine, more popularly called the Fatah, is one of the organizations that played a major role in the conflict. The organization was founded in 1959 by Yasser Arafat and some others, and from that point, it has played a forefront role in the military and political efforts of Palestine.

The organization originally emerged as a reaction to the displacement and suffering of Palestinian citizens in the aftermath of the war that led to the creation of the state of Israel in 1948. It was originally a guerrilla militant organization with the purpose of resisting and recovering Israeli occupation of Palestinian territories.

This organization recorded some form of progress and gained dominance within the Palestine Liberation Organization - a coalition of Palestinian groups aimed at representing the people of Palestine - in the 1960s and 1970s. That led to them becoming recognized within the Palestinian political space and in international communities.

The prominence of Fatah was cemented in 1970 when the PLO (Palestine Liberation Organization), with Fatah as its leading faction, achieved international recognition and observer status at the United Nations. This was a significant milestone as it solidified the PLO and Fatah's role as a key player in the quest for Palestinian self-determination.

However, in 1988, the PLO, led by Fatah, recognized Israel's right to exist, renounced terrorism, and marked a major milestone in the Israeli-Palestinian conflict. This move by the PLO and Fatah paved the way for a series of negotiations with Israel, which led to the Oslo Accords of 1993, where Fatah, represented by the PLO, signed the Oslo Accords with Israel. These accords laid the foundation for the establishment of the Palestinian Authority (PA), granting limited self-governing powers in parts of the West Bank and Gaza Strip.

After the signing of the Oslo Accords and the formation of the Palestinian Authority, Yasser Arafat, the de facto leader of the Fatah organization, became the first president of the PA in 1994. That became a significant development in the quest for Palestinian self-governance, and it marked a transition from armed resistance to a more diplomatic approach, although tensions persisted.

At that time, it felt like these two nations were gradually reaching a consensus, but the early 2000s introduced the Second Intifada, a violent Palestinian uprising against Israeli occupation. In this period of the second intifada, the relationship between the Israeli government and Fatah became strained once again, and this led to bloodshed, loss of lives and properties, and hardships for both parties.

In 2004, after the death of Yasser Arafat, Mahmoud Abbas became the new leader of Fatah and the Palestinian Authority, and he continued to negotiate with Israel, emphasizing the two-state solution as the path to peace.

Over time, Fatah's role in the Israeli-Palestinian conflict has evolved from its early days as a guerrilla organization to a more diplomatic and politically oriented entity. Fatah sought to represent the Palestinian citizens through negotiations and diplomatic efforts in their quest for self-determination and a peaceful resolution. However, the path to lasting peace remains a complex and ongoing process, marked by numerous challenges and setbacks.

Also, unity efforts between Fatah and Hamas, another major Palestinian faction, have been marked by complexities. In 2011, they signed a reconciliation agreement, but implementing it effectively has been challenging due to deep-seated differences. That leads us to our next power player - the Hamas.

HAMAS: ISLAMIC RESISTANCE MOVEMENT

Hamas, or the Islamic Resistance movement, was founded in 1987 during the first intifada, a time of Palestinian uprising against Israeli rule. This body presented itself as an alternative to Fatah - which is more politically oriented and is the dominant force within the Palestine Liberation Front.

While the Fatah posed as an organization that believed in diplomatic and peaceful resolution of conflict, the Hamas movement took a hard stand. The most significant milestone in its history was when it won the Palestinian Legislative elections in 2006. This win handed the control of the Palestinian Legislative Council to Hamas, and by extension, it also got control of the Gaza Strip.

In the year 2007, Hamas forcibly took control of the Gaza Strip, further deepening the divide between them and Fatah (which retained control of the West Bank). This forceful takeover of the Gaza Strip was another major event marked in the Israeli-Palestinian conflict, and it led to long-lasting consequences.

From its inception, Hamas's stance towards Israel has been marked by its refusal to recognize Israel as a legitimate state or entity. Therefore, it engaged in regular armed exchanges with Israel, launching rocket attacks and sometimes engaging in clashes along the Gaza-Israel border.

There have been many efforts geared towards reconciling Fatah and Hamas, but they have all been fruitless largely because Hamas refused to adjust its stance. In 2012, the two factions signed a reconciliation agreement, but its implementation was faced with significant hurdles. Also, in 2014, a unity government was formed, but the deep-seated political and ideological differences between the two groups quickly nullified the government. The division between these two major Palestinian factions remains a significant challenge to achieving Palestinian unity and a negotiated resolution to the conflict.

Hamas's control of Gaza since 2007 has come with various challenges. It has administered the Gaza Strip, maintaining security and providing services, but has also faced an Israeli blockade, which Israel maintains for security reasons. The organization has also alternated between armed resistance against Israel and temporary ceasefire agreements. Various international mediators, including Egypt, Qatar, and the United Nations, have brokered these ceasefires.

THE ISRAELI GOVERNMENT'S ROLE IN THE ISRAELI-PALESTINIAN CONFLICT

On the Palestinian side of the conflict, we've seen the contributions of players like the Fatah and Hamas. On the Israeli side of the conflict, the major player will be the Israeli government itself.

The new and Modern State of Israel became an entity after its official declaration and establishment on May 14, 1948. This independence declaration sparked a new war between Israel and the neighboring states, culminating in drastic changes in territorial landmarks, loss of life on both sides and the displacement of Palestinian Arabs in particular. The Israeli leadership wanted a government of their own, and they snatched it in the way they thought they could.

After the 1948 war and the declaration of the state of Israel, the conflict persisted, and it blew up again in 1967, leading to the Six-Day War. This Six-day War led to Israel occupying and taking control of East Jerusalem, the Gaza Strip, the West Bank, and some other territories, further fueling the fire of the already bloody conflict.

That continued until 1978, during the Camp David Accords that the United States of America brokered. The 1978 Camp David

Accords was the first significant attempt at negotiating peace between Israel and its neighbors, and it saw them sign a peace treaty with Egypt - the first Arab country to recognize Israel's right to exist.

Furthermore, in what came to be known as the Oslo Accords of 1993, there was an improvement in the relationship between the Israeli government and the Palestinian leadership. This accord led to the establishment of the Palestinian Authority (PA) and granted limited self-governing powers to Palestinians in parts of the West Bank and Gaza Strip.

This new relationship ultimately led to Israel withdrawing from the Gaza Strip in 2005. During this time, the Israeli government dismantled their settlements, withdrew and evacuated civilians, and handed the Gaza Strip over to the Arabs.

While this was a crucial step towards peace, Israel maintained control of Gaza's borders and airspace. Therefore, when Hamas took over Gaza in 2007, Israel imposed a blockade on the territory. The blockade was originally meant to restrict the flow of weapons and materials that could be used for military purposes, but it affected Gaza's economy and humanitarian situation.

During the years that followed 2010, there were various rounds of peace negotiations involving the Israeli Government and the Fatah-led Palestine Liberation Organization, but these did not necessarily lead to permanent peace within the region.

THE UNITED STATES ROLE IN THE ISRAELI-PALESTINIAN CONFLICT

While there have been major involvements in the conflict by local entities like the Fatah and others that we've talked about, we can't underestimate the influence of external entities like the United States of America in this unsolved conflict.

One of the first noticeable involvements of the United States in the Israeli-Palestinian conflict came in 1948 when it established diplomatic relations with the newly formed State of Israel. Thus, becoming one of the first countries to recognize the existence of Israel as an independent Nation. The U.S.'s support for Israel was rooted in shared democratic values and, later, strategic considerations in the Middle East.

The U.S. government also played a crucial role during and after the Six-Day War in 1967, providing military and diplomatic support to Israel, and it also helped broker the Camp David Accords between Israel and Egypt in 1978, leading to the first-ever peace treaty between Israel and an Arab nation, where Egypt officially recognized Israel's right to exist for the first time.

After brokering the Camp David Accords, the U.S. was also central to the Oslo Accords in 1993. These two accords, in 1978 and 1993, marked a significant step toward achieving peace in the Israeli-Palestinian conflict by establishing the framework for the Palestinian Authority (PA) and limited Palestinian self-governance to the West Bank and Gaza Strip.

From the 1990s to the early 2000s, the U.S. was actively involved in peace negotiations between Israel and the Palestinian Authority. However, despite efforts like the Camp David Summit in 2000, these negotiations did not result in a final peace agreement.

In 2002, the U.S. government, along with the United Nations, European Union, and Russia, introduced the Roadmap for Peace. This Roadmap outlined some steps aimed at resolving the conflict. This Roadmap for peace included the creation of an independent Palestinian state.

Furthermore, in 2005, the U.S. supported Israel's unilateral withdrawal from the Gaza Strip 2005, which included the dismantling of Israeli settlements. However, Israel maintained control of Gaza's borders and airspace, and the United States also continued to provide military support and economic aid to Israel, reinforcing its commitment to Israel's security. In 2016, the U.S. pledged a historic $38 billion in military assistance to Israel over ten years.

In 2017, further showing its support for the State of Israel, the United States made a significant and controversial move when it officially relocated its embassy in Israel from Tel Aviv to Jerusalem in 2017. This decision was met with international criticism and protests by Palestinians.

In its entirety, The United States' role in the Israeli-Palestinian conflict is heavily marked by its support for Israel's security, mediation of peace negotiations, and involvement in regional diplomacy.

THE UNITED NATIONS' ROLE IN THE ISRAELI-PALESTINIAN CONFLICT

The United Nations is yet another player in the Israeli-Palestinian conflict. It played an essential role in the early stages of the conflict by adopting the UN Partition Plan in 1947. This partition plan proposed the division of Mandatory Palestine under the British Administration into separate Jewish and Arab states, with Jerusalem under international administration. As we learned in the first chapter, when we explored their history, this proposition was accepted by Jewish leaders while it was rejected by the Palestinian Arabs, leading to the independence war of 1948.

The next significant UN involvement in the conflict was in 1950 when it established the United Nations Relief and Works Agency for Palestine Refugees in the Near East (UNRWA). The UNRWA was established to provide ongoing assistance to Palestinian refugees and their descendants, who were displaced during the independence war.

In the aftermath of the Six-Day War in 1967, the UN became involved in the conflict once again when it passed Resolution 242, which called for Israel's withdrawal from territories it occupied during the war and for a just settlement of the refugee problem. This resolution effort would go on to become a cornerstone for future peace efforts in the region. Furthermore, in 1974, the UN General Assembly granted the Palestine Liberation Organization (PLO) non-member observer status, recognizing it as the representative of the Palestinian people, marking a significant shift in the UN's approach to the conflict.

In 2012, the UN General Assembly voted to grant non-member observer state status to the State of Palestine. And its Security Council adopted numerous resolutions related to the Israeli-Palestinian conflict, addressing issues such as settlements, the status of Jerusalem, and the situation in Gaza. Additionally, the UN has been involved in peacekeeping missions in the region, like the United Nations Truce Supervision Organization (UNTSO) and the United Nations Interim Force in Lebanon (UNIFIL).

Outside of peacekeeping efforts and efforts at conflict resolution, the UN has been actively involved in providing humanitarian aid to Palestinians living in conflict-affected areas, particularly in Gaza. Agencies like the United Nations International Children's Emergency Fund (UNICEF) and the United Nations Relief and Works Agency for Palestine refugees (UNRWA) have played significant roles in delivering essential services to those in need.

The United Nations has also consistently advocated for a two-state solution as the path to peace in the Israeli-Palestinian conflict. This solution envisions the coexistence of Israel and a future Palestinian state side by side, living in peace and security.

Essentially, this body's role in the Israeli-Palestinian conflict has been multifaceted, encompassing diplomacy, peacekeeping, humanitarian aid, and advocacy for a two-state solution, and it continues to be a critical component of international efforts aimed at finding a lasting and equitable resolution to this protracted conflict.

THE EUROPEAN UNION'S ROLE IN THE ISRAELI-PALESTINIAN CONFLICT

The European Union's contribution to the Israeli-Palestinian conflict began to gain significance in the 1980s and 1990s when it focused on supporting the Middle East peace process and providing financial aid to Palestinians in the West Bank and Gaza Strip. The European Union (EU) was also one of the co-sponsors of the Madrid Conference in 1991, and this marked the launch of the first direct negotiations between Israel and its Arab neighbors, including Palestinians, after the Gulf War.

When the Oslo Accords was signed by the conflicting parties in 1993, the EU became a significant donor to the Palestinian Authority (PA). It committed substantial financial aid to help build Palestinian institutions and promote economic development, and in 1995, the EU and Israel signed an Association Agreement aimed at strengthening political and economic ties. However, the agreement included a human rights clause, which allowed the EU to suspend parts of the agreement in the event of human rights violations.

Also, in 1995, The EU initiated the Euro-Mediterranean Partnership (also known as the Barcelona Process). This partnership was to enhance regional cooperation, peace, and stability in the Mediterranean region, and it included efforts to address the Israeli-Palestinian conflict.

The EU adopted a clear position against Israeli settlements in the occupied Palestinian territories. It deemed the settlements illegal under international law and has regularly called for a freeze on settlement construction and established the European Union Border Assistance Mission for the Rafah Crossing Point in Gaza in 2005. This mission aimed to facilitate the movement of people and goods to and from Gaza and Egypt.

Furthermore, several European Union member states, like Sweden, Ireland, and Luxembourg, recognized the State of Palestine in 2014, and the European Parliament passed a non-binding resolution in 2014 calling for the recognition of Palestinian statehood, although the EU as a whole did not formally adopt this position.

The EU, like the United Nations, has consistently advocated for a two-state solution to the Israeli-Palestinian conflict, with Israel and Palestine living side by side in peace and security, and it continues to support diplomatic initiatives aimed at achieving this goal.

THE ARAB LEAGUE'S ROLE IN THE ISRAELI-PALESTINIAN CONFLICT

The Arab League is a regional organization comprising Arab states, and it has played a notable role in the conflict. Established in 1945, just before the end of World War II, with the goal of promoting economic, cultural, and political cooperation among Arab states, the Arab League quickly became deeply involved in regional political issues, particularly the Israeli-Palestinian conflict.

In 1947, when the UN adopted the partition plan for Palestine, The Arab League, along with Arab states, opposed the plan, leading to the 1947-1949 Arab-Israeli War. In the years that followed the war, between the 1950s and 1960s, the Arab League actively supported Palestinian nationalist movements and the establishment of the Palestine Liberation Organization (PLO) in 1964.

The Arab League played a pivotal role during and after the Six-Day War in 1967. The Arab League has consistently supported the establishment of an independent Palestinian state, with East Jerusalem as its capital, based on the 1967 borders. It has also called for an end to Israeli settlements in the West Bank. Following Israel's occupation of the West Bank, East Jerusalem, Gaza Strip, and other territories, the Arab League convened the Khartoum Summit in Sudan, where Arab states declared the "Three No's": no recognition, no peace, and no negotiations with Israel. However, it relaxed this stance a bit in 2002 when it adopted the Arab Peace Initiative, which offered comprehensive peace, normalization of relations, and recognition of Israel in exchange for its withdrawal from occupied territories and a just solution to the Palestinian refugee issue.

Arab League summits have provided a platform for Arab states to coordinate their positions on the Israeli-Palestinian conflict. Diplomatic initiatives, negotiations, and peace proposals have been key features of these gatherings.

Aside from the political aspects of its dealings, The Arab League has also provided financial assistance to Palestinians in the form of humanitarian aid and development projects in the

West Bank, Gaza Strip, and Palestinian refugee camps and has maintained relations with the United Nations, the European Union, and the United States to seek international support for the Palestinian cause and promote peace efforts.

THE ROLE OF OTHER MIDDLE EASTERN STATES IN THE ISRAELI-PALESTINIAN CONFLICT

While the Israeli-Palestinian conflict primarily involves Israel and Palestine, other Middle Eastern states have also played one role or another over the years. These states often aligned themselves with one side or the other and contributed to diplomatic initiatives or influenced the conflict in different ways. Some of these states are Jordan, Egypt, Lebanon, Syria, and Iran, among others.

- **Jordan and Egypt**

After the 1948 Independence War, Jordan annexed the West Bank, while Egypt took control of the Gaza Strip. This marked a period of Jordanian and Egyptian rule in these territories, which lasted until the Six-Day War in 1967.

In 1979, Egypt became the first Arab state to sign a peace treaty with Israel, normalizing diplomatic relations, and in 1994, Jordan followed suit, signing a peace treaty with Israel, which remains in effect today. These treaties have been instrumental in shaping the regional dynamics of the conflict.

- **Lebanon**

Lebanon was deeply affected by the presence of the Palestine Liberation Organization (PLO) and became a battleground for various factions involved in the conflict. The 1975-1990 Lebanese Civil War was marked by Israeli interventions and Syrian involvement, further complicating the regional landscape.

Also, in southern Lebanon, the militant group Hezbollah, backed by Iran and Syria, periodically engaged in hostilities with Israel, and these violent exchanges have had an impact on the broader regional context.

- **Syria**

In the 1967 Six-Day War, Israel gained control of Golan Heights and occupied it. That act has been a source of sustained tension between Israel and Syria, and the region is a focus of conflict with evident implications for the central Israeli-Palestinian conflict.

Also, Syria provided support to Palestinian groups, both politically and militarily, in their struggle against Israel. Syrian support, in combination with Iranian backing, has been a key factor in the dynamics of the conflict.

- **Iran**

Speaking of Iran, it has been a consistent supporter of groups that oppose Israel, such as Hezbollah in Lebanon and various Palestinian factions. Its funding, military aid, and political backing have played a role in shaping the conflict's dynamics.

Over the course of the conflict, Iran's leaders have maintained a hostile stance towards Israel, often calling for its destruction. Thus, contributing to regional tensions and conflicts.

- **Saudi Arabia and the Gulf States**

Some Gulf states, led by Saudi Arabia, have supported peace initiatives aimed at resolving the Israeli-Palestinian conflict. They have also promoted economic development projects in the Palestinian territories.

For example, in 2020, the United Arab Emirates (UAE) and Bahrain signed normalization agreements with Israel, known as the Abraham Accords. These agreements marked a significant shift in regional dynamics and sparked debate about the future of the conflict.

Generally speaking, the involvement of other Middle Eastern states in the Israeli-Palestinian conflict has been complex, with each state pursuing its interests and policies. These states have often been influenced by regional rivalries and alliances, making their roles in the conflict multifaceted and, at times, contradictory.

THE ROLE OF NON-GOVERNMENTAL ORGANIZATIONS (NGOS)

The Israeli-Palestinian conflict has drawn the attention of numerous non-governmental organizations (NGOs) that aim to provide humanitarian aid, advocate for human rights, and contribute to peace-building efforts. One such body is the United Nations Relief and Works Agency (UNRWA).

The United Nations Relief and Works Agency for Palestine Refugees in the Near East was established in 1950 to provide assistance to Palestinian refugees and their descendants displaced during the 1948 Arab-Israeli war.

Today, UNRWA continues to provide essential services, including education, healthcare, and food assistance to Palestinian refugees in the West Bank, Gaza Strip, Jordan, Lebanon, and Syria.

Many NGOs, such as the International Committee of the Red Cross (ICRC), Médecins Sans Frontières (Doctors Without Borders), and the Oxford Committee for Famine Relief (Oxfam), have been active in the Palestinian territories. They provide humanitarian aid, medical care, and development programs to mitigate the impact of conflict and occupation.

Aside from the NGOs mentioned earlier, human rights organizations like Amnesty International have also been monitoring and reporting on human rights abuses, advocating for the rights of Palestinians, and highlighting the impact of the conflict on civilians. Also, Israeli NGOs like B'Tselem document human rights violations in the occupied territories, focusing on the impact of Israeli policies on Palestinian communities.

Organizations like OneVoice are another body that has contributed to the conflict in their way by aiming to promote grassroots activism for a peaceful two-state solution and engaging Palestinians and Israelis in dialogue and coexistence initiatives.

Another organization, Combatants for Peace, founded in 2005, works towards bringing together former Israeli and Palestinian fighters who have renounced violence to advocate for a peaceful resolution to the conflict.

Palestinian NGOs like Al-Haq have worked to address legal issues and advocate for Palestinian rights in international forums, often using international law as a framework for their advocacy.

The Breaking the Silence organization, comprising former Israeli soldiers, collects testimonies from soldiers who have served in the occupied territories, shedding light on the realities of military occupation.

The Geneva Initiative is a joint Palestinian-Israeli NGO that promotes a detailed peace plan, engaging politicians, civil society, and the public in peace-building efforts.

The Peres Center for Peace and Innovation, founded by former Israeli President Shimon Peres, aims to promote regional cooperation and peace-building initiatives, including cross-border healthcare programs.

Seeds of Peace brings together young leaders from conflict regions, including Israeli and Palestinian youths, to engage in dialogue and build bridges of understanding. An organization like The Hand in Hand, a network of bilingual schools in Israel, brings Jewish and Arab students together to promote coexistence, tolerance, and education for peace.

All of these NGOs have been pivotal in addressing the humanitarian needs of Palestinians, advocating for human rights, and promoting peace and coexistence in the Israeli-Palestinian conflict. They have collectively impacted the lives of individuals in the region and contributed to the international discourse on this protracted conflict.

THE ROLE OF CIVIL SOCIETY IN THE CONFLICT

Civil society, comprising individuals, organizations, and movements outside of government structures, plays a crucial role in the Israeli-Palestinian conflict. These actors often pursue grassroots initiatives, advocate for peace, and address the humanitarian needs of affected communities.

One such society is the Palestinian National Movement of the Late 19th Century. This movement emerged in response to increasing Jewish immigration and land purchases in Palestine, with early activism focusing on preserving Palestinian identity and land rights.

Another society is the Peace Now movement. Founded in 1978, this Israeli organization was one of the earliest peace movements advocating for a two-state solution, withdrawal from occupied territories, and an end to settlements.

Palestinian civil society organizations began to form in the 1980s, focusing on various aspects of community development, education, and human rights, and they played a significant role in the First Intifada, a largely non-violent popular uprising against Israeli occupation. During this period, local committees organized protests, strikes, and civil disobedience.

After the first intifada, the Second Intifada saw civil society organizations and grassroots movements on both sides engage in protests, advocacy, and initiatives for peace, although the conflict escalated into violence. In the midst of these, the West Bank village of Bil'in, Gaza became known for its weekly nonviolent protests against the Israeli separation barrier, attracting international attention.

Founded in Jerusalem in 1988, the Women in Black group holds silent vigils, advocating for an end to violence and the establishment of a Palestinian state, while groups like the Combatants for Peace and The Parents Circle comprise former Israeli and Palestinian fighters and bereaved families, respectively. These groups work together to promote peaceful resolution, dialogue, and cooperation.

The Legal Center for Arab Minority Rights in Israel, founded in 1996, is another group civil society group. It advocates for the rights of Arab citizens in Israel, including issues related to discrimination and land confiscation. While a prominent Palestinian human rights organization, Al-Haq focuses on legal advocacy, documenting violations of international law, and addressing issues related to the occupation.

International Solidarity Movements is also one of the civil society groups that has contributed to the Israeli-Palestinian conflict. This global network brings international activists to the West Bank and Gaza Strip to engage in nonviolent activism, including accompanying Palestinian farmers during olive harvests.

The BDS movement (Boycott, Divestment, Sanctions movement), launched in 2005, calls for international pressure on Israel to end the occupation, grant equal rights to Palestinian citizens, and acknowledge the rights of Palestinian refugees. It has gained significant international attention and sparked debates on the ethics and effectiveness of boycotts.

All these civil society actors often work to bridge divides, build understanding, and address the humanitarian needs of affected communities, making a significant impact on the conflict's dynamics and discourse.

THE ROLE OF PUBLIC OPINION

Public opinion is a powerful and often underestimated factor in the Israeli-Palestinian conflict. The views, perceptions, and sentiments of people around the world, as well as those within the region, significantly influence policies, negotiations, and the trajectory of the conflict.

For example, the international community's reaction to the UN Partition Plan, which proposed the division of Palestine into separate Jewish and Arab states, was marked by both support and opposition. Jewish leaders embraced the plan, while Arab states and Palestinians largely rejected it. This led to a clash of opinions, ultimately culminating in a blown-out war.

Also, the events surrounding the 1948 war led to the displacement of hundreds of thousands of Palestinian Arabs, creating a refugee crisis and shaping public opinion on both sides of the conflict. The plight of Palestinian refugees became a focal point for Arab and Palestinian narratives, emphasizing their right to return to their homeland.

Furthermore, the outcome of the Six-Day War in 1967, which resulted in Israel's occupation of the West Bank, Gaza Strip, and other territories, further fueled Arab and Palestinian grievances and the founding of Peace Now, an Israeli organization advocating for a two-state solution and the end of settlements marked the emergence of peace movements within Israel.

The largely non-violent nature of the First Intifada garnered international support and shifted perceptions of Palestinians from passive victims to active participants in their quest for self-determination.

Egypt's peace treaty with Israel in 1979 and Jordan's peace treaty in 1994 brought regional recognition of Israel and had a considerable impact on public opinion in these countries. The Arab Peace Initiative, which offered normalization of relations with Israel in exchange for its withdrawal from occupied territories, reflected a shift in regional perceptions and was seen as a potential path to peace.

The conflict's portrayal in the media, as well as social media, has a profound impact on public opinion. Images and stories from the region can quickly shape international perceptions. Also, global solidarity movements, like the International Solidarity Movement (ISM), bring international activists to the West Bank and Gaza to participate in nonviolent resistance and draw attention to the conflict.

In essence, public opinion in the Israeli-Palestinian conflict is a dynamic and evolving force that influences policies, negotiations, and the international response to the conflict. The diverse range of narratives, emotions, and perspectives surrounding the conflict reflects its complexity and the ongoing challenge of finding a just and lasting resolution.

THE DOMINO EFFECT: UNDERSTANDING THE SOCIO-ECONOMIC IMPACT OF THE CONFLICT

The long-standing conflict, with the recent declaration of the "state of war" by Israel as it goes arms-on-arms against Hamas - a Palestinian militant organization - has affected and continues to affect the region and neighboring nations on various levels. From politics to the economy to the everyday lives of the average citizens of these nations, the effect of this conflict has been profound and unfortunate. The sad part is that these promises will continue to aggravate unless a resolution is reached as soon as possible.

For example, Palestinians in the West Bank and Gaza are faced with many obstacles in their daily lives. Checkpoints, road closures, and the imposing separation barrier significantly hinder their ability to commute, whether for work, education, or healthcare. Over time, these restrictions have effectively become barriers to accessing job opportunities and essential services.

THE WEIGHT OF WAR: ECONOMIC STRUGGLES FACED BY ISRAELIS AND PALESTINIANS

In this enduring Israeli-Palestinian conflict, the economic landscape is as complex and contentious as the political one. Decades of instability have taken a heavy toll on the economic well-being of both Israelis and Palestinians.

- **The Effect of Conflict**

On one side of the conflict, the Palestinian territories grapple with persistently high unemployment rates, with the youth bearing the brunt of this burden. A scarcity of job opportunities within the territories forces many Palestinians to seek employment in Israel or overseas, leading to a brain drain that exacerbates the economic challenges.

Also, the Palestinian Authority relies heavily on foreign aid to sustain its economy, and while this international assistance is crucial for addressing immediate needs, it leaves the Palestinian economy vulnerable to fluctuations in international political priorities. In addition to these, the blockade on Gaza, a response to security concerns, has created a humanitarian crisis. It imposes severe restrictions on imports and exports, stifling businesses and hindering reconstruction efforts. The blockade's consequences continue to cast a long shadow, affecting the economy and well-being of Gazans.

On the other side, Israel's unique security situation necessitates substantial defense and security spending. As much as it is understandably essential, this allocation of resources diverts funding that could otherwise be invested in economic development and social welfare. The protracted conflict demands continuous investment in defense and emergency preparedness. This sustained expenditure hinders the redirection of resources toward long-term economic growth.

Despite boasting a prosperous economy, Israel contends with significant economic disparities. A high cost of living and income inequality present pressing challenges that demand attention for a more equitable society.

The conflict also disrupts trade between Israel and the Palestinian territories, effectively limiting economic growth. Mutual economic dependency persists, but it remains fraught with complications. The ever-present risk associated with the conflict discourages both foreign and domestic investment in the region. The conflict's shadow looms large, creating a significant obstacle to sustainable economic development and also creating immediate economic problems.

Another part of the economic effect of the conflict is the periodic escalations, armed exchanges, clashes, and wars that lead to the destruction of infrastructures on the sides of all involved parties. When these vital infrastructures are destroyed, the need to rebuild constitutes a costly undertaking that further strains the economy of the nations and the region at large.

- **Opportunities for Economic Growth**

In the midst of these hostilities, there lies untapped potential for regional cooperation. Collaborative economic ventures and partnerships between Israelis and Palestinians have the power to pave the way for mutual prosperity. This spirit of collaboration can bolster economic resilience and stimulate growth.

Suppose these conflicting nations can prioritize education and vocational training programs. In that case, they can empower the region's youth, equipping them with the skills needed to compete in the job market and alleviate the persistent problem of high unemployment.

Additionally, if successful, efforts to diversify economies in both Israel and Palestine can make their economic systems more resilient and adaptable to challenges. Given the region's strategic location, there is significant potential for greater regional integration in trade and infrastructure development. This could bring economic benefits to all parties involved.

In essence, the Israeli-Palestinian conflict has left both Israelis and Palestinians grappling with profound economic challenges. While these struggles persist, opportunities for economic growth and cooperation abound. If a resolution is reached and these parties can address the economic burdens that weigh on their communities and foster a spirit of collaboration, a brighter, more prosperous future can be envisioned, even in the face of ongoing political tensions.

- **Education and Conflict: The Challenge to Learn Amid Unrest**

In the midst of the Israeli-Palestinian conflict, education stands as a fundamental right and a powerful tool that should be accessible to all. However, this longstanding conflict, marked by political instability and violence, poses significant challenges to the education of Palestinian and Israeli children.

- **The Problem**

The conflict has resulted in frequent disruptions to the normal academic calendar. Schools in the West Bank and Gaza Strip have faced closures, often due to violence or security concerns, leaving students with intermittent access to education. For Palestinian students, this has led to substantial learning gaps, particularly for younger generations.

The conflict has taken a toll on educational infrastructure. Schools, a place that should provide safety and stability, have often become targets or collateral damage. This destruction limits access to safe and functional learning spaces for Palestinian students. which is detrimental to their prospects for quality education.

Outside the issue of infrastructure, both Israeli and Palestinian communities are experiencing a shortage of trained and qualified teachers. This scarcity affects the quality of education. Palestinian students, in particular, often have to make do with educators of varying expertise levels, which can result in subpar learning outcomes.

Also, the conflict subjects students on both sides to psychological trauma. Palestinian children living in the West Bank and

Gaza Strip experience the trauma of conflict and occupation. On the Israeli side, communities near the Gaza Strip often suffer from rocket attacks, leading to trauma among students. These psychological scars hinder the ability to learn and succeed academically.

The Israeli-Palestinian conflict has tragically seen the recruitment of child soldiers. These children are deprived of their right to an education and are often subjected to violence, leaving them with few opportunities for a better future. Schools, besides being centers of learning, play a pivotal role in fostering social cohesion and community resilience. The conflict disrupts this social fabric and can have long-lasting effects on Palestinian and Israeli communities as they are torn apart by political violence.

On both sides of the conflict, the lack of access to quality education can perpetuate the cycle of poverty. Also, families and communities suffer from reduced opportunities for economic advancement as generations struggle to access quality education. Thus, the domino effect continues from the economy to education and back to a ripple effect on the economy.

- **Efforts to Overcome the Challenges**

In response to conflict-related disruptions, many organizations and communities have sought alternative learning methods. These include radio programs, distance learning, and online education, which have been used to reach students on both sides of the conflict.

Also, recognizing the trauma faced by students, many organizations have sought to provide psychosocial support and counseling services to help Palestinian and Israeli students cope with the psychological toll of the conflict.

There are also international initiatives and organizations advocating for the protection of students, teachers, and educational facilities during times of conflict. This includes the Safe Schools Declaration, which promotes the safety and security of educational spaces.

Additionally, these local and international organizations are creating awareness of the importance of education regardless of the situation of things. Education holds the potential to shape attitudes and values. By promoting tolerance, diversity, and peaceful coexistence within curricula, education can play a role in mitigating the drivers of the Israeli-Palestinian conflict.

These organizations understand that education nurtures future leaders. When Palestinian and Israeli students are exposed to inclusive and conflict-sensitive curricula, they are better equipped to address the root causes of the conflict and advocate for peaceful solutions. An educated populace is often more resilient in the face of conflict. Education provides individuals with a better understanding of their rights, access to information, and critical thinking skills that enable them to navigate difficult circumstances.

Education is a fundamental right that should transcend the conflict's darkness. By addressing the unique challenges faced by Palestinian and Israeli students and embracing the potential of education as a tool for conflict resolution, there is a brighter future where education prevails even amid the most challenging circumstances.

HEALTH AND CONFLICT: THE STRUGGLE FOR WELL-BEING

The conflict has undeniably affected every aspect of life in the region. Asides from its effect on education and the economy, it has also left a profound impact on the health and well-being of the populace in the region. As a conflict characterized by sporadic violence, political instability, and ongoing tensions, the provision of adequate healthcare is an ongoing challenge.

Achieving sustainable peace in the Israeli-Palestinian conflict will require a focus on health, as well as other social determinants. Ensuring that healthcare is accessible and of high quality can contribute to the well-being of communities and offer them a stake in the peace process.

- **Challenges to Health in the Israeli-Palestinian Conflict**

The Israeli-Palestinian conflict has resulted in physical and administrative barriers that limit access to healthcare services for Palestinian communities. Checkpoints, road closures, and other security measures create difficulties in reaching medical facilities, leading to delayed or inadequate care. The available health facilities have also not been spared in this protracted conflict. Hospitals and clinics in the Gaza Strip and the West

Bank have faced destruction, making it even more challenging for Palestinians to access healthcare. The damage inflicted on healthcare infrastructure leads to a reduced capacity to provide essential services.

Both Palestinian and Israeli communities suffer from the psychological trauma of conflict. Palestinian children living in the West Bank and Gaza Strip experience the trauma of conflict and occupation. Communities near the Gaza Strip are exposed to rocket attacks, leading to psychological trauma among Israelis. This trauma, if left unaddressed, can have severe long-term implications on mental health.

Outside of the mental health issue posed by this conflict, there's also the disruption of vaccination programs, increasing the vulnerability of children to preventable diseases. Additionally, the disruption of access to vaccines for children is enhanced by the regular destruction of healthcare infrastructure and restricted movement of medical personnel.

In both Palestinian territories and Israel, there are shortages of healthcare personnel, medicines, and medical equipment. These shortages hinder the capacity of the healthcare system to respond effectively to the healthcare needs of the population.

The health challenges posed by the conflict have severe economic consequences for communities on both sides. For example, the health expenditures of households increase due to the unavailability of adequate public healthcare services, leaving families grappling with the financial burden of accessing private healthcare.

Also, healthcare workers on both sides of the conflict face enormous stress and risk. They work tirelessly to provide care in difficult and often dangerous conditions. This strain can lead to burnout and negatively impact the quality of care provided. Sometimes, these healthcare professionals can be caught in the line of fire and end up losing their lives.

- **Efforts to Improve the Health Situation in the Region**

There have been continued efforts to improve the healthcare situation in the Israeli-Palestinian region. For example, numerous international organizations and humanitarian groups provide healthcare services to Palestinians in the West Bank and Gaza Strip. These organizations help fill the gaps in the healthcare system by offering essential medical services and humanitarian assistance.

There are also several initiatives dedicated to providing mental health support to communities affected by the conflict. These programs aim to address the trauma and emotional distress experienced by both Palestinians and Israelis.

The promotion of health diplomacy, with a focus on joint projects and shared resources, can serve as a pathway to improve the well-being of populations on both sides of the conflict. Collaborative efforts to tackle common health challenges could build trust and cooperation. Initiatives that promote cooperation in healthcare can serve as a confidence-building measure. By jointly addressing healthcare challenges,

Palestinians and Israelis can develop trust, potentially spilling over into broader peace efforts.

In addition, addressing the health disparities in the region can significantly enhance living conditions for both Palestinians and Israelis. Improved health outcomes could lead to a more stable and secure environment.

In the midst of the Israeli-Palestinian conflict, the struggle for well-being continues. Providing healthcare and addressing the health challenges facing both Palestinians and Israelis is essential for mitigating the humanitarian toll of this ongoing conflict. By recognizing the profound impact of health and well-being on the lives of individuals and communities, the warring region can move closer to a future in which the well-being of the populace is safeguarded.

EVERYDAY LIFE AMID CONFLICT: THE STRUGGLE FOR NORMALCY

The Israeli-Palestinian conflict casts a long shadow over the daily lives of millions in the region. Amid this protracted conflict, the quest for normalcy has become a paramount struggle for both sides.

- **Education Disrupted**

Education plays a vital role in the lives of young Palestinians and Israelis. However, conflict-related disruptions, including curfews, military checkpoints, and violence, often prevent children from attending school. As a result, students from both sides can experience interrupted learning, hindering their educational development.

For Palestinian children in the West Bank and Gaza, attending school is a daily challenge. Military checkpoints, road closures, and the risk of violence on the way to school create an environment where education is anything but routine.

In Israel, communities near the Gaza Strip face the constant threat of rocket attacks, causing repeated school closures and psychological distress among children.

- **Economic Uncertainty**

The conflict's economic repercussions affect the daily life of both Israelis and Palestinians. In Israel, communities within rocket range of the Gaza Strip face significant economic challenges. The need to run for shelter during rocket attacks disrupts work and daily routines.

In the Gaza Strip, where unemployment is high, securing stable employment is a daily concern. Economic difficulties translate into uncertainty for families and individuals.

- **Mobility and Access**

Mobility is a major concern for Palestinians living in the West Bank and Gaza Strip. Roadblocks, checkpoints, and restrictions on movement make everyday activities like commuting to work, visiting family, or accessing healthcare a daunting task.

Palestinians in the West Bank may need to go through numerous checkpoints to reach their destinations, leading to delays, humiliation, and frustration.

- **Healthcare Struggles**

The Israeli-Palestinian conflict has placed considerable strain on healthcare services in the region. Both Palestinians and Israelis grapple with challenges to their healthcare needs.

In the Gaza Strip and the West Bank, conflict-related damage to healthcare infrastructure has resulted in reduced access to medical care. In Israel, communities near the Gaza Strip contend with the psychological trauma of repeated rocket attacks, impacting their mental health.

- **Daily Fear and Resilience**

Living in a conflict zone means coping with the constant fear of violence. Both Israelis and Palestinians adapt to the presence of conflict in their lives, and resilience becomes a daily necessity.

In southern Israel, the "Color Red" warning system alerts residents to incoming rocket attacks. While this system provides some protection, it also reminds residents of the ever-present threat. In the Gaza Strip, families have constructed safe rooms in their homes, creating small sanctuaries where they can take refuge during rocket attacks.

- **Efforts to Reclaim Normalcy**

Despite the harsh realities they face, individuals and communities on both sides of the Israeli-Palestinian conflict make efforts to lead normal lives. In Israel, communities near the Gaza Strip have established support networks to help each other through difficult times. The spirit of communal solidarity is vital in maintaining a semblance of normal life. In the West Bank and Gaza Strip, cultural events and initiatives bring communities together. Art, music, and literature offer an escape from the harshness of everyday life.

The Israeli-Palestinian conflict presents daily challenges to the lives of those in the region. The quest for normalcy has become a testament to the resilience and determination of both Israelis and Palestinians to live their lives despite the conflict.

In a conflict characterized by its long history and deep-rooted tensions, the pursuit of normalcy is not just an everyday struggle but an extraordinary act of resilience in the face of adversity. The people caught in this protracted conflict demonstrate their strength and determination to reclaim their lives and assert their right to a normal existence.

LOOKING FORWARD: THE SOCIO-ECONOMIC FUTURE AMID CONFLICT

The conflict's economic consequences are far-reaching. The inability to find a peaceful resolution often results in economic stagnation, limiting opportunities for both Israelis and Palestinians.

In the Gaza Strip, the unemployment rate hovers at around 50%, leaving many families struggling to make ends meet. The blockade and periodic conflicts make it difficult for the local economy to grow. In Israel, communities near the border with Gaza face challenges as well. Small businesses can be forced to close during escalations, leading to financial instability. Despite the ongoing challenges and adversities faced by both Israelis and Palestinians, it's crucial to explore potential pathways for a more stable and prosperous future.

- **Investment in Infrastructure and Development**

One way to pave the way for a better future is through increased investment in infrastructure and development. By improving the socio-economic conditions, it is possible to create a more stable environment conducive to peace.

In the West Bank and Gaza, infrastructure projects could lead to job creation and a boost in the local economy. Improved transportation networks and better access to markets can help businesses thrive.

In Israel, communities near conflict zones can benefit from targeted investments aimed at strengthening their resilience. Supporting local businesses and infrastructure can help these communities flourish even in the face of challenges.

- **Youth Engagement and Education**

Engaging with the younger generation is essential for any future peace process. By providing quality education and economic opportunities, we can help build a better future for all.

In the West Bank and Gaza, investing in education and providing young people with the skills they need for future employment is crucial. Empowering youth can lead to a more stable society. In Israel, supporting educational initiatives in conflict-prone areas can help young people feel more secure about their future, even in the face of adversity.

- **Cross-Border Economic Initiatives**

Creating cross-border economic initiatives can foster cooperation and mutual dependence between Israelis and Palestinians. Joint economic projects and trade agreements can help build trust and reduce hostility. For example, there could be joint ventures in agriculture, technology, or tourism.

In Israel, supporting initiatives that foster cross-border cooperation can lead to economic benefits and improved relations with their Palestinian neighbors.

- **International Engagement and Diplomacy**

A lasting socio-economic transformation in the region also requires continued international engagement and diplomatic efforts. The international community has an essential role in promoting economic development and peace in the region. By providing economic aid and diplomatic support, they can facilitate much-needed progress.

International organizations can help facilitate dialogue between the conflicting parties, encouraging them to find peaceful resolutions to their differences.

- **Community Resilience and Grassroots Initiatives**

Local communities play a significant role in shaping their socio-economic future. Grassroots initiatives and community resilience can contribute to improved conditions and hope for a more stable environment.

In the Gaza Strip and the West Bank, local organizations can provide support and resources to vulnerable communities, fostering their resilience in the face of economic challenges. In Israel, communities near the border with Gaza have demonstrated remarkable resilience. By supporting and empowering these communities, they can become centers of growth and stability.

Despite the complex and enduring nature of the Israeli-Palestinian conflict, there are opportunities for improving the socio-economic conditions in the region. By investing in infrastructure, youth education, cross-border initiatives, and diplomatic solutions, stakeholders can create a path towards a brighter future for all.

The journey toward socio-economic improvement is a collective effort that requires the engagement of the international community, local communities, and individuals on both sides of the conflict. Together, they can shape a more hopeful and prosperous future, even amid the ongoing challenges of the Israeli-Palestinian conflict.

THE POLITICAL CHESSBOARD: UNDERSTANDING THE ISRAEL-PALESTINE POWER PLAY

*W*e can't take away politics from the dynamics of a nation. After all, the political atmosphere is what determines the kind of leaders the nation will have and the decisions the nation might take. That is no less different in the case of Israel and Palestine and their longstanding conflict. To that end, we will explore the political playground of the Israeli and Palestinian nations and how they have affected the ongoing conflict. We'll also explore other external political players and their influence as we try to chart a course for a better understanding of the conflict toward reaching a lasting resolution.

POLITICAL IDEOLOGIES: THE FOUNDATIONS OF THE CONFLICT

One thing that we have hammered over and over in the course of the book is the need to look at the conflict from way back instead of just skimming over shallow waters. In that vein, we would like first to explore the political ideologies of the two nations, how they are interwoven, and how they contributed to the aggravation or otherwise of this ongoing and longstanding conflict that has seen the parties facing significant losses and consequences at different intervals.

- **The 20th Century and the furtherance of conflict**

Within Israel and Palestine's intertwined political landscape, the Balfour Declaration of 1917 stands as a critical document in the Israeli-Palestinian conflict. Issued by the British government, this declaration marked a significant endorsement of the establishment of a "national home for the Jewish people" in Palestine. Its ramifications would reverberate through the 20th century, setting the stage for increased Jewish immigration to Palestine under British mandate.

Simultaneously, the 20th century bore witness to the emergence of Arab nationalism as a potent force. Arab leaders, troubled by the prospect of a Jewish state in Palestine, vehemently opposed the Balfour Declaration and the concurrent surge in Jewish immigration. The clash of these two nationalistic movements ignited the flames of a conflict that would shape the destiny of the region.

The gruesomeness of the Holocaust became a catalyst for a renewed commitment to the Zionist cause. The international community, grappling with the moral imperative to address the suffering of Jewish survivors and the historical injustices perpetrated against them, began to support the idea of a Jewish state. The urgency to provide a haven for survivors and prevent the reoccurrence of such laid the groundwork for the post-war discussions on the future of Palestine.

In this context, the Balfour Declaration gained renewed significance. The British government, recognizing the shifting tides of global sentiment, found itself navigating the complexities of post-war geopolitics. The declaration, once a commitment to Zionist aspirations, now assumed a role in the broader narrative of post-Holocaust restitution and the recognition of the Jewish people's right to self-determination.

The aftermath of World War II propelled the issue of Jewish immigration to the forefront of international discourse. The plight of displaced Jews and the moral imperative to address historical injustices led to increased support for the establishment of a Jewish state. This momentum ultimately resulted in the United Nations' endorsement of the partition plan in 1947, a proposal that sought to create independent Jewish and Arab states in Palestine.

In that year, the international community proposed a partition plan that envisaged the creation of separate Jewish and Arab states, with Jerusalem designated as a global city. While the Jewish leadership accepted this plan, seeing it as a pathway to the establishment of the State of Israel, Arab leaders vehemently rejected it, setting the stage for further conflict. The year 1948 witnessed the culmination of tensions with the declaration of the State of Israel. The immediate aftermath was the eruption of the Arab-Israeli War, a conflict that would significantly shape the trajectory of the region. Arab states, rejecting the very existence of Israel, launched an invasion, leading to a protracted and devastating conflict. This period also marked what Palestinians refer to as the Nakba, meaning "catastrophe" in Arabic. Hundreds of thousands of Palestinians either fled or were expelled from their homes during this time, creating a complex and enduring refugee crisis.

The declaration of the State of Israel and the subsequent Arab-Israeli War laid the foundation for the entrenched hostilities and territorial disputes that characterized the Israeli-Palestinian conflict. The Nakba remains a poignant and profoundly resonant term in Palestinian history, encapsulating the profound losses and displacement experienced by the Palestinian people during this period.

The 1960s brought a notable evolution in the Palestinian struggle with the establishment of the Palestinian Liberation Organization (PLO). Initially oriented towards armed resistance, the PLO underwent a significant transformation, shifting its focus to advocating for Palestinian self-determination. This ideological shift marked a nuanced approach, emphasizing diplomatic and political strategies alongside the historical armed struggle.

The PLO's evolution reflected broader changes in the geopolitical landscape, with a growing international recognition of the Palestinian cause. The organization emerged as a key player, representing Palestinian interests on the global stage. The transition from a primarily militant stance to a diplomatic approach reflected the maturation of the Palestinian national movement and its adaptation to the complexities of international relations.

The 1960s were essential in shaping the narrative of the Israeli-Palestinian conflict, introducing elements that would define the dynamics for decades to come. The conflict moved beyond a regional dispute to become a matter of global concern, drawing attention to the complexities of national aspirations, statehood, and the quest for self-determination in a deeply contested land. It became a fully blown political and diplomatic matter.

The outcome of the Six-Day War in 1967 was another crucial point in the Israeli-Palestinian conflict. Israel, in a swift and decisive military campaign, occupied the West Bank, East Jerusalem, and the Gaza Strip. This occupation had far-reaching consequences, reshaping the geopolitical landscape and introducing new dynamics to an already complex conflict.

One significant outcome of the post-1967 era was the establishment of Israeli settlements in the occupied territories. The construction of these settlements, seen by many as a direct violation of international law, intensified tensions between Israelis and Palestinians. From the Palestinian perspective, these settlements were viewed as significant impediments to the realization of their aspirations for statehood. The issue of settlements became a focal point of contention, as it not only altered the demographic and geographic reality on the ground but also became a major stumbling block in peace negotiations.

The settlements, often strategically positioned, served both political and security purposes for Israel. However, they became a source of deep resentment and frustration among Palestinians, fueling a sense of dispossession and exacerbating the conflict.

The 1990s witnessed ushered in a new phase in the political landscape with the signing of the Oslo Accords. This agreement between Israel and the Palestine Liberation Organization (PLO) was aimed at paving the way for a two-state solution, fostering mutual recognition and cooperation. The Oslo Accords raised hopes for a resolution to the longstanding conflict, offering a framework for negotiations and the establishment of the Palestinian Authority.

However, the Oslo Accords faced substantial challenges and setbacks, casting a shadow over the prospects of lasting peace. One of the primary obstacles was the continued expansion of Israeli settlements in the West Bank, a direct contradiction to the spirit of the peace process. The expansion of settlements and disputes over the status of Jerusalem became critical points of contention, undermining the goodwill generated by the Oslo framework.

The 1990s, despite the optimism generated by the Oslo Accords, revealed the entrenched complexities of the Israeli-Palestinian conflict. The promises of a two-state solution faced the harsh realities of geopolitical shifts, security concerns, and deeply ingrained historical narratives. The Oslo Accord, rather than heralding a definitive resolution, marked a phase of both promise and disillusionment, setting the stage for the ongoing challenges that persist in the quest for a just and lasting peace in the region.

POLITICAL PARTIES: THE KEY PLAYERS

In this intricate and interwoven story of two nations in an unending clash, the political parties on both sides have played and continue to play a crucial role in shaping policies, influencing public opinion, and ultimately constituting a significant force in the trajectory of the ongoing conflict. Thus, we need to look at these key players (or political parties) and understand their influence and impact on the escalation and de-escalation of the conflict.

- **Israel: A Multifaceted Political Landscape**

On the Israeli side of the conflict, many political parties have had their say in the culmination of war or attempts at resolution. Some of these parties include the Likud Party, the Kadima, and the Labor Party, among others.

- **Likud Party**

Founded in 1973, the Likud party has been an essential player in shaping Israel's political landscape. This party was initially formed as a merger of several right-wing parties, and it advocates for a strong security stance, emphasizing an uncompromising approach to regional conflicts. Over the years, the Likud

Party has been associated with a conservative agenda and a commitment to the expansion of Israeli settlements in the West Bank, a contentious issue in the peace process. Key leaders of the Israeli community, including Benjamin Netanyahu, have been prominent figures within Likud, influencing policies and negotiations with the Palestinians.

- **Kadima**

Established in 2005 by then-Prime Minister Ariel Sharon, Kadima emerged as a centrist political force aiming to advance the peace process. The party positioned itself as a pragmatic alternative to more conservative factions, advocating for the evacuation of certain settlements as part of a negotiated two-state solution. Despite its initial prominence, Kadima faced internal challenges and a decline in influence in subsequent years.

- **Labor Party**

This party is one of the oldest political parties in Israel. It has a rich history that is deeply intertwined and as old as the foundation of the state of Israel. Historically associated with the peace process, The Labor Party has undergone ideological shifts and internal divisions.

While some leaders within the party continue to emphasize a commitment to a two-state solution, the overall influence of the Labor Party has diminished compared to its earlier prominence in shaping Israeli policies.

- **Blue and White**

Another notable political party within the Israeli political landscape is the Blue and White Party. A more recent entrant into the political arena, Blue and White, was formed in 2019 as a centrist coalition led by former Chief of General Staff Benny Gantz.

The party aims to provide an alternative to Likud, focusing on issues such as good governance, social welfare, and national security. Blue and White's formation reflected a desire for a pragmatic and centrist approach to address the challenges facing Israel.

PALESTINE: A COMPLEX MOSAIC

As it is on the Israeli side of the conflict, so it is on the Palestinian side. The Palestinians also boast of a number of political organizations responsible for influencing the conflict. Whether seeking a peaceful resolution or a hardline stance, each of these parties or organizations has been essential to the direction of the conflict.

- **Fatah**

Founded in the 1950s, Fatah has been a dominant political force in the Palestinian Authority (PA). Led by Mahmoud Abbas, Fatah has engaged in peace negotiations with Israel, advocating for a two-state solution. However, internal divisions and challenges to Fatah's leadership have complicated its ability to present a unified front, impacting its effectiveness in navigating the complex political landscape.

- **Hamas**

Hamas, founded in the late 1980s, is a multifaceted organization with both political and militant wings. With an Islamist ideology, Hamas gained popularity for its resistance to Israeli occupation. Its charter calls for the establishment of an Islamic state in historic Palestine. Since taking control of the Gaza Strip in 2007, Hamas has become a significant player, challenging Fatah's influence and further complicating the Palestinian political scene.

- **Islamic Jihad Movement in Palestine**

While smaller in size compared to Fatah and Hamas, the Islamic Jihad Movement is a noteworthy player, particularly in Gaza. Sharing ideological similarities with Hamas, it advocates for the establishment of an independent Palestinian state. The group has played a role in shaping the dynamics of the conflict and influencing the trajectory of events in the region.

- **Popular Front for the Liberation of Palestine (PFLP)**

Founded in 1967, the PFLP is a leftist organization with a history rooted in armed struggle. Although its influence has waned over the years, the PFLP remains active in Palestinian politics, emphasizing resistance and rejecting peace talks without what it considers significant concessions. The PFLP's ideological stance contributes to the diversity of political perspectives within the Palestinian territories.

The interplay between Israeli and Palestinian political parties is dynamic and shaped by historical grievances, security concerns, and conflicting visions for the future. The evolving nature of political parties on both sides adds to the intricacy of the peace process. Navigating these complexities is crucial for comprehending the ongoing challenges and prospects for resolution in the Israeli-Palestinian conflict.

POLITICAL PROCESSES: NAVIGATING THE MAZE

To wrap up our exploration of the political landscape of these conflicting nations, let's look at their political processes to understand the conflict further and point out potential ways to conflict resolution.

ISRAEL'S POLITICAL PROCESSES: ELECTIONS AND COALITION BUILDING

Israel's democratic system is a labyrinth of political intricacies, playing an essential role in shaping the nation's stance on critical issues, including the Israeli-Palestinian conflict. In Israel's political landscape, elections are the way that the leaders and members of governance are decided.

The country employs a proportional representation electoral system, distinguishing it from the individual-focused systems found in many other democracies. Here, citizens cast their votes for political parties, each of which competes for seats in the 120-member Knesset.

Elections in Israel are frequent, with citizens actively participating in choosing their representatives. However, the system's complexity arises from the diversity of parties, each championing its distinct ideology and policy agenda.

Winning an outright majority in the Knesset is a rare feat, often leading to coalition governments. The negotiation and compromise required for coalition building have a direct impact on policy directions, especially concerning issues as sensitive as the Israeli-Palestinian conflict.

The role of the Prime Minister is central to Israel's political dynamics. Traditionally, the leader of the party securing the most seats in the Knesset is invited to form a government. The Prime Minister wields considerable influence, shaping policies and, by extension, the nation's approach to pressing matters like national security and peace negotiations. The political ideology and diplomatic understanding of the Prime Minister can significantly alter the trajectory of Israel's relationship with the Palestinians.

Policy-making in Israel involves a multifaceted process encompassing government institutions, security agencies, and the military. The Knesset, Israel's legislative body, serves as the forum for debating and approving policies. Its committees play a crucial role in shaping the legislative agenda. Policy-makers must navigate the complex interplay of security considerations, public opinion, and international relations, mainly when crafting strategies related to the Israeli-Palestinian conflict.

- **Palestine's Political Processes: A Struggle for Unity**

In a visibly sharp contrast to Israel's relatively stable political landscape, the Palestinian territories grapple with internal divisions that have lasting implications for their engagement with Israel. The West Bank is governed by the Fatah-led Palestinian Authority (PA), while the Gaza Strip is under the control of the militant group Hamas. This political schism has profound consequences, presenting challenges in presenting a unified Palestinian front in negotiations with Israel.

The division in leadership, with competing authorities in the West Bank and Gaza, complicates efforts to reach a comprehensive agreement. The lack of a singular, authoritative voice hampers the effectiveness of Palestinian negotiators and undermines their ability to present a cohesive strategy. The political divide exacerbates the challenges in fostering unity among the Palestinian people, a crucial factor in achieving lasting peace.

Elections, a cornerstone of democratic governance, have faced significant hurdles in the Palestinian territories. The last presidential elections were held in 2005, and attempts to conduct subsequent parliamentary elections encountered delays and setbacks.

The absence of a regular and inclusive electoral process contributes to a leadership vacuum, fostering a sense of political stagnation. The question of representation, encompassing diverse political voices, remains a critical challenge that necessitates a comprehensive and inclusive electoral approach.

The involvement of international actors further complicates the Palestinian political landscape. Organizations such as the United Nations and neighboring countries exert influence, adding a layer of complexity to decision-making processes.

External pressures, aid dynamics, and diplomatic efforts play a significant role in shaping the policies of Palestinian leaders. Balancing the expectations of the international community by addressing the needs and aspirations of the Palestinian people is an ongoing challenge that shapes the course of negotiations and conflict resolution.

The interplay between Israeli and Palestinian political processes is a critical factor in the dynamics of the Israeli-Palestinian conflict. Achieving progress in the peace process necessitates effective communication, negotiation, and a commitment to addressing the aspirations and concerns of both Israeli and Palestinian populations.

The ongoing complexities in political processes highlight the need for sustained efforts and international cooperation to navigate the intricate path toward a resolution.

While Israel's democratic system and coalition politics bring diversity to decision-making, the division between Fatah and Hamas and the absence of regular elections in the Palestinian territories pose significant challenges. Bridging these gaps and fostering unity within the Palestinian leadership is crucial for presenting a coherent strategy in negotiations with Israel.

As the political processes continue to evolve, the need for comprehensive understanding, dialogue, and diplomatic efforts becomes increasingly pronounced. The road to resolution is fraught with obstacles, but navigating the complexities of Israeli and Palestinian political landscapes is an indispensable step toward achieving lasting peace in the region.

THE CURRENT STATE OF AFFAIRS: UNDERSTANDING RECENT DEVELOPMENTS

We've gone through the history of this longstanding conflict, we've examined the history and contributions of the different moving parts in the cog of the wheel driving the conflict, and we have finally gotten to a point where we have a fairly solid understanding of the dynamics of the conflict. However, this conflict is an ongoing one, so we need to look at the current state of things and understand recent developments. When we consider the retrospective aspects of the conflict and blend them with the recent happenings, we'll reach an even better understanding, and we might finally get to a point where we can make more viable solution propositions. Therefore, we'll be dedicating this chapter to taking a holistic view of the recent happenings surrounding the Israeli-Palestinian conflict, starting with the Trump Era and how it shifted the policy of the United States of America concerning the conflict.

THE TRUMP ERA: A SHIFT IN AMERICAN POLICY

The tenure of Donald Trump as the president of the United States of America left an indelible mark on the Israeli-Palestinian conflict, ushering in a series of policy adjustments that disrupted longstanding diplomatic conventions. The period was marked by controversial decisions and strategic realignments, and it shaped the dynamics of the conflict and elicited diverse reactions on the global stage.

One of the notable moments of the Trump Era came on December 6, 2017, when President Trump declared the official recognition of Jerusalem as the capital of Israel. This move was a stark departure from decades of international consensus, and it reverberated through the region and beyond.

While the Israeli side of the conflict readily and understandably welcomed this acknowledgment of Jerusalem as its 'undivided' capital, the Palestinian side, alongside some Arab leaders and the majority of the international community, opposed the move. Their primary contention lay in the status of East Jerusalem, considered by Palestinians as the future capital of their sovereign state. This move by president Trump set the tone for subsequent policy shifts, underscoring the Trump administration's pro-Israel stance.

Following the acknowledgment by the Trump administration, the United States solidified its commitment by relocating its embassy from Tel Aviv to Jerusalem on May 14, 2018. The timing, coinciding with the 70th anniversary of Israel's establishment, underscored the administration's determination to align its policies with Israel's positions. While the move was celebrated in Israel, it triggered widespread protests and condemnation in the Palestinian territories and across the Arab world.

The Trump administration adopted a tough stance against what it perceived as a lack of commitment from the Palestinian leadership to engage in meaningful peace negotiations. In 2018, the United States announced a substantial reduction in funding to the United Nations Relief and Works Agency for Palestine Refugees (UNRWA), citing financial inefficiency and a desire for burden-sharing among contributors. Simultaneously, the administration ordered the closure of the Palestine Libera-tion Organization (PLO) office in Washington, citing the Pales-tinian Authority's refusal to participate in peace talks.

In continued support for Israel, on January 28, 2020, President Trump, alongside Israeli Prime Minister Benjamin Netanyahu, unveiled the long-anticipated "Peace to Prosperity" plan, collo-quially known as the "Deal of the Century." The plan proposed a two-state solution but with significant territorial adjust-ments, the recognition of a demilitarized Palestinian state, and a concept of "conditional sovereignty" for Palestinians. While Israel welcomed the plan, Palestinian leaders rejected it because they saw it as biased and detrimental to their national aspirations.

Furthermore, a remarkable geopolitical shift occurred with the signing of the Abraham Accords in 2020. Brokered by the

Trump administration, these agreements marked the normalization of diplomatic relations between Israel and the United Arab Emirates (UAE) and Bahrain. While it was celebrated as a historic breakthrough, critics contended that the process bypassed the longstanding Palestinian question and risked undermining Arab solidarity.

Proponents of the Trump approach lauded the administration's boldness in challenging established norms, fostering regional partnerships, and prioritizing Israeli security. However, critics, including many within the international community, argued that the policies overlooked the rights and aspirations of the Palestinian people, making it challenging to achieve a just and lasting resolution to the conflict.

In essence, the Trump era introduced a paradigm shift in U.S. policy on the Israeli-Palestinian conflict. The series of decisions, from recognizing Jerusalem as Israel's capital to unveiling a controversial peace plan and brokering normalization agreements, continues to influence the complex dynamics of the conflict. The implications of these policies persist, shaping the prospects for future negotiations and the pursuit of a comprehensive resolution.

THE ABRAHAM ACCORDS: A NEW DIRECTION FOR MIDDLE EAST DIPLOMACY

Proposed and brokered by the Trump Administration, the Abraham Accords was a transformative force that reshaped the diplomatic landscape of the Middle East. These agreements marked a significant departure from traditional diplomatic norms and triggered a cascade of reactions on the global stage.

The historic ceremony marking the Abraham Accords unfolded on the White House on September 15, 2020. At this event, representatives from Israel, the United Arab Emirates (UAE), and Bahrain gathered to sign the Abraham Accords. This momentous event marked the formal normalization of diplomatic relations between Israel and the two Gulf nations. The accords were hailed as groundbreaking, representing the first time Arab nations normalized ties with Israel since Jordan in 1994 and Egypt in 1979.

The Abraham Accords signified a departure from the long-standing Arab consensus on the normalization of the relationship with Israel on the resolution of the Israeli-Palestinian conflict. The UAE and Bahrain broke this tradition by normalizing relations without waiting for a comprehensive resolution of the Palestinian issue. This shift reflected a pragmatic recalibration of priorities, with a focus on shared economic, security, and technological interests.

One of the prime focuses of the Abraham Accords was the emphasis on economic cooperation and technological collaboration. The signatory nations recognized the mutual benefits of forging stronger economic ties. As a result, there was an influx of investments and joint ventures, fostering collaboration in areas such as finance, healthcare, and technology. The agreements opened up new horizons for the participating nations, signaling a departure from the constraints of historical animosities.

Beyond economic cooperation, the Abraham Accords also forged a strategic alliance against common regional threats. Iran's regional influence and its nuclear ambitions emerged as shared concerns, creating a foundation for security collaboration. The signatory nations and the United States formed a united front to address regional challenges, enhancing stability in the process.

The Abraham Accords was successful in its own right, and its success resonated beyond the initial signatories. Building on the momentum, Morocco and Sudan also normalized relations with Israel in subsequent months. These expansions underscored the potential for a new era of diplomatic engagements in the Middle East, with nations choosing to prioritize mutual interests over historical grievances.

However, while the Abraham Accords received acclaim for fostering regional stability and cooperation, reactions were mixed. Some lauded the agreements as a diplomatic breakthrough that could pave the way for broader Middle East peace. Others, particularly Palestinian leadership, criticized the accords for sidestepping the longstanding issue of Palestinian statehood.

Regardless of the sides to the story, the Abraham Accords represented a seismic shift in Middle East diplomacy, challenging conventional norms and fostering unprecedented cooperation. As the region navigates this new chapter, the enduring impact of these accords on regional dynamics and the quest for a comprehensive resolution to the Israeli-Palestinian conflict remains a subject of global attention.

THE ISRAELI POLITICAL SCENE: A PERIOD OF INSTABILITY

The already complex Israeli political landscape has been thrown into a state of heightened turbulence in the recent events concerning the Israeli-Palestinian conflict. The intricate interplay of historical grievances, security challenges, and shifting alliances has rendered the political scene particularly volatile, with key developments shaping the nation's trajectory.

In the latest developments at the time this writing (November 2023), Israel finds itself grappling with a surge in tensions in the Israeli-Palestinian conflict. The year started with a series of violent incidents, including clashes in the West Bank and military operations in response to perceived security threats. The cyclical nature of violence in the region has placed immense pressure on the Israeli political leadership to navigate through uncharted waters.

The political landscape underwent a significant transformation with the establishment of a new coalition government on December 29, 2022. Led by Prime Minister Benjamin Netanyahu, this coalition comprises six parties, including the Religious Zionist Party, which holds a position emphasizing national religious values. The inclusion of this party has raised concerns about its stance on the Israeli-Palestinian conflict, particularly in relation to settlements in the West Bank.

The coalition agreements carry commitments that include the advancement and development of settlements, even in the contentious West Bank. This stance, coupled with recent authorizations for settlements in the West Bank, has intensified the debate around the government's approach to the peace process and its willingness to engage in meaningful dialogue.

On February 13, 2023, the Israeli government's Security Cabinet authorized the establishment of nine settlements in the occupied West Bank. This move, characterized as a response to what was labeled as "murderous terrorist attacks" in east Jerusalem, drew swift international reactions. The U.N. Security Council issued a presidential statement expressing concerns about the potential hindrance to peace and the viability of a two-state solution.

In response, the Israeli Prime Minister's Office dismissed the U.N. statement as "one-sided," asserting that the United States should not have joined it. The subsequent announcement of a temporary pause in building new settlements for the coming months indicated a response to international pressure, showcasing the delicate balancing act that the Israeli government must undertake in its pursuit of domestic security and international relations.

In the face of intensifying violence, Israeli and Palestinian delegates, alongside U.S. and Egyptian officials, made a joint commitment on February 26, 2023, to take immediate steps to quell the surge. The commitment, which was forged in Aqaba, Jordan, included a cessation of unilateral measures for a period of three to six months. However, there were doubts regarding the feasibility of these joint commitments, with key figures, including the finance minister and chair of the Religious Zionist Party, rejecting certain elements, such as the settlement freeze.

In all of these, the international community, led by the United Kingdom, has been proactive in addressing the conflict. The U.K.'s statements at the U.N. Security Council underscored the importance of restoring stability and urged both parties to de-escalate tensions. The U.K., along with the US, France, Germany, and Italy, issued a joint statement in February 2023, reaffirming their commitment to a comprehensive, just, and lasting peace in the Middle East.

Also, the United Nations, through various agencies and envoys, has consistently called for the resolution of the conflict, emphasizing the urgent need to address core issues fueling the conflict. U.N. Secretary-General António Guterres highlighted the necessity for regional and international collaboration to break the cycles of violence and restore calm.

On the domestic front, the Israeli government faces the challenge of fostering unity amid diverse political ideologies and opinions on the conflict. The recent outbreak of violence triggered by Israeli settlers and subsequent responses from both the Prime Minister and the Israel Defense Forces underscores the complexities of maintaining internal stability.

As Israel navigates this period of political turbulence, the trajectory of the Israeli-Palestinian conflict remains unpredictable. The delicate balance between domestic security concerns, international relations, and internal unity adds layers of complexity to an already intricate political landscape. The coming months will likely shape the course of political events, determining whether the region moves towards sustained peace or further entrenches itself in the quagmire of conflict.

THE GAZA CONFLICTS: A CYCLE OF VIOLENCE AND ITS HUMANITARIAN IMPACT

In the midst of the Israeli-Palestinian conflict, one of the most volatile flashpoints is the Gaza Strip. This densely populated enclave has been at the center of numerous conflicts. In recent years, the region has experienced a troubling cycle of violence with severe humanitarian implications.

The Gaza Strip is a narrow coastal territory wedged between Israel and Egypt and has been a focal point of contention since the establishment of the State of Israel in 1948. Over the years, the region has witnessed conflict, mass displacements, and a complex web of geopolitical maneuvering.

In 2023, the Gaza Strip once again became a battleground, with escalations in violence adding to the longstanding grievances of the Palestinian population. The conflict, marked by rocket attacks from Gaza and Israeli airstrikes, escalated tensions to a level not seen since previous clashes. The trigger for this round of violence was multifaceted, involving contested land, political dynamics, and historical animosities.

The toll on civilians caught in the crossfire has been devastating, as the Gaza Strip has seen a significant number of casualties, including civilians, women, and children. The intensity of the conflict has strained the already fragile infrastructure, exacerbating the humanitarian crisis. As the conflict unfolded, reports of civilian casualties poured in from both sides.

The densely populated landscape of Gaza meant that airstrikes, even if targeted, often resulted in collateral damage. The toll on human lives, with innocent civilians paying the price, highlighted the tragic consequences of the ongoing hostilities.

In these recent series of conflicts and wars in the region, displacement became a harsh reality for many Gazans. Families, already grappling with economic hardships and political uncertainties, found themselves forced to flee their homes in search of safety. The displacement crisis further burdened the limited resources available, with makeshift shelters struggling to accommodate the influx of those seeking refuge.

The conflict has taken a severe toll on Gaza's infrastructure. Essential services such as hospitals, schools, and water facilities have been damaged or destroyed, pushing the region into a dire humanitarian situation. The destruction of critical infrastructure not only hampers immediate relief efforts but also poses long-term challenges for the community's recovery.

Beyond the tangible destruction, the conflict in the Gaza Strip leaves a lasting mark on the mental and emotional well-being of the affected population. The constant fear of airstrikes, the loss of loved ones, and the uncertainty of the future contribute to a pervasive sense of trauma. The psychosocial impact of the conflict extends beyond the immediate violence, casting a shadow on the mental health of individuals and communities.

The international community, alarmed by the escalating violence and humanitarian crisis, has called for an immediate cessation of hostilities. Various world leaders and organizations have expressed concern over the impact on civilian lives and have urged both parties to prioritize diplomatic solutions over military actions, and various media houses have been doing their best to bring the horrors of the ongoing conflict and wars to the limelight.

Humanitarian aid has become a crucial lifeline for the affected population. International organizations and NGOs are working tirelessly to provide medical assistance, shelter, and necessities to those in need. However, the challenges are immense, given the constraints imposed by the ongoing conflict.

The recurring conflicts in the Gaza Strip underscore the urgent need for a comprehensive and sustainable peace plan. The cycle of violence perpetuates a dire humanitarian situation, and without addressing the root causes, the region remains trapped in a seemingly endless loop of hostilities.

As the international community grapples with the aftermath of the recent Gaza conflicts, the urgent call for lasting peace echoes louder than ever. Addressing the humanitarian crisis requires not only immediate relief efforts but also a commitment to addressing the root causes of the Israeli-Palestinian conflict. Until a comprehensive and inclusive peace plan is implemented, the people of Gaza will continue to bear the brunt of the recurring violence, caught in a cycle that denies them the stability and security they deserve.

THE WEST BANK: ONGOING SETTLEMENT EXPANSION AND ITS IMPLICATIONS

In recent years, the expansion of Israeli settlements in the West Bank has emerged as a contentious issue, adding layers of complexity to the already intricate geopolitical landscape and the ongoing tussle between the Israelis and the Palestinians.

The West Bank, a landlocked territory nestled between Israel and Jordan, holds immense historical and cultural significance for both Israelis and Palestinians. It encompasses key religious sites, including Jerusalem, and has been a focal point of contention since the 1967 Six-Day War when Israel occupied the region.

One of the critical dynamics shaping the conflict is the persistent expansion of Israeli settlements in the West Bank. These settlements, viewed as illegal under international law, are constructed on land claimed by Palestinians for a future independent state. The expansion involves not only the construction of new settlements but also the growth of existing ones, altering the demographic and geographic realities on the ground.

The timeline of settlement expansion provides insight into the evolving dynamics:

1. Post-1967: In the aftermath of the Six-Day War, Israel began establishing settlements in the West Bank and East Jerusalem, areas it had occupied. The

construction of settlements was a strategic move,
intertwining security concerns, political objectives,
and a vision of Greater Israel.

2. 1978: The Camp David Accords saw the establishment
   of the first Israeli settlement, Ofra, in the West Bank.
   The move was met with international criticism,
   setting the stage for decades of disputes over
   settlement expansion.

3. 1990s: The Oslo Accords, aimed at fostering peace,
   envisioned the creation of a Palestinian state.
   However, the period also witnessed a surge in
   settlement construction, complicating the peace
   process.

4. 21st Century: Settlement expansion continued, with
   new constructions and population growth in existing
   settlements. The expansion was met with
   condemnations from the international community,
   including the United Nations.

The expansion of Israeli settlements has far-reaching consequences for the Palestinian population in the West Bank.

Palestinians view the settlements as encroachments on their
land and a major obstacle to the establishment of a viable
Palestinian state. The expansion often involves the confiscation
of Palestinian-owned land, leading to disputes and legal
battles.

On the economic side of things, the settlements control crucial
resources, including water and fertile land, impacting Pales-

tinian agriculture and economic activities. The economic disparities between settlers and Palestinians contribute to tensions and grievances.

Also, the physical presence of settlements and the infrastructure connecting them restrict the movement of Palestinians, creating fragmented enclaves. Checkpoints, roadblocks, and the separation barrier further complicate daily life for Palestinians in the West Bank.

The international community, through various resolutions and statements, has consistently condemned Israeli settlement expansion. For example, multiple U.N. resolutions, including UNSC Resolution 242 and 338, deem the Israeli settlements as violations of international law. The resolutions call for the withdrawal of Israeli forces from occupied territories, including the West Bank.

The International Court of Justice (ICJ), in its advisory opinion, declared the construction of Israeli settlements in the occupied Palestinian territories, including the West Bank, as contrary to international law.

Leaders and diplomats from around the world, including European nations and the United States, have also expressed concerns over settlement expansion and have continuously called for a freeze on settlements as part of broader efforts to revive peace negotiations.

This ongoing settlement expansion by the Israelis in the West Bank poses a significant challenge to the broader peace process between Israelis and Palestinians. For instance, the internationally endorsed two-state solution envisions an independent and viable Palestinian state coexisting with Israel. However, the expansion of settlements altering the demographics and geography of the West Bank makes the realization of this vision increasingly difficult.

Also, this continuous settlement expansion in the West Bank by the Israelis erodes trust and confidence between the parties, complicating any attempts at meaningful negotiations as Palestinians perceive the ongoing construction as a deliberate attempt to preclude the establishment of their sovereign state.

The issue of settlement expansion in the West Bank remains a critical juncture in the Israeli-Palestinian conflict. Resolving this complex challenge requires not only diplomatic efforts but a genuine commitment from both sides to engage in negotiations that address the core issues. Until a comprehensive and mutually acceptable resolution is reached, the settlement expansion will continue to cast a shadow over the prospects of a just and lasting peace in the region.

THE PALESTINIAN AUTHORITY: POLITICAL DIVISIONS AND CHALLENGES

In this complex and intertwined story of conflict between two nations, the Palestinian Authority (P.A.) stands as a key player, grappling with internal divisions and external challenges. Established through the Oslo Accords in the 1990s, the Palestinian Authority was envisioned as an interim self-governing body, yet its journey has been marked by political complexities and hurdles.

The Oslo Accords, negotiated between Israel and the Palestine Liberation Organization (PLO) in the early 1990s, laid the groundwork for the creation of the P.A. The accords aimed at fostering a transitional period during which the Palestinians would progressively assume self-governance in the West Bank and Gaza Strip. However, the envisioned trajectory toward statehood faced numerous roadblocks.

The political landscape within the Palestinian territories is characterized by a longstanding rivalry between Fatah and Hamas, the two dominant political factions.

- **Fatah:** Historically associated with the PLO and its leader, Yasser Arafat, Fatah took the reins of the newly formed P.A. Mahmoud Abbas, Arafat's successor, assumed leadership, steering Fatah's agenda towards negotiations with Israel. Fatah remains a central force within the P.A., advocating for a two-state solution through diplomatic channels.

- **Hamas:** In contrast, Hamas, an Islamist movement founded in the late 1980s, has grown in prominence. Winning parliamentary elections in 2006, Hamas's victory led to a rupture in Palestinian politics. The group, which rejects the existence of Israel, controls the Gaza Strip, creating a divided governance structure. The ongoing tension between Fatah and Hamas significantly impacts the efficacy of the P.A.

The Palestinian Authority grapples with internal challenges that impede effective governance and erode public confidence. Over the years, allegations of corruption within the P.A. have surfaced, contributing to a sense of disillusionment among Palestinians. The mismanagement of funds and accusations of nepotism have fueled discontent, posing a substantial hurdle to the P.A.'s credibility.

The absence of presidential elections since 2005 and internal disputes over leadership have also raised questions about the P.A.'s legitimacy. The failure to hold regular elections further compounds the challenges of representative governance and accountability.

The Palestinian Authority faces intricate external dynamics, with its actions and decisions influenced by both regional and international factors. One contentious issue is the security coordination between the P.A. and Israel. While such cooperation is aimed at maintaining stability and preventing violence, it has sparked criticism from Palestinians, who view it as collaboration with an occupying force. Thus, balancing security concerns with public sentiment remains a delicate challenge for the Palestinian Authority.

Another problem faced by the Palestinian Authority is that it is heavily reliant on international aid for financing. Donor countries and organizations provide substantial financial support, but this dependence also exposes the P.A. to external pressures. The fluctuating nature of international aid adds an element of uncertainty to the P.A.'s economic and political landscape.

In the midst of all of these, the P.A.'s approach to the Israeli-Palestinian conflict reflects a blend of diplomatic efforts and a commitment to resistance.

Fatah, as the leading faction within the P.A., has consistently pursued a diplomatic approach, engaging in peace talks and seeking international recognition. Efforts to gain recognition for Palestinian statehood and condemnation of Israeli settlements on the global stage are part of this strategy.

Hamas, controlling Gaza, adheres to a resistance narrative, emphasizing armed struggle against Israeli occupation. The divergent approaches between Fatah and Hamas contribute to the complexity of representing a unified Palestinian stance.

As a crucial body to the Palestinians and the Palestinian struggles, the Palestinian Authority stands at a crossroads, facing multifaceted challenges as it strives to navigate the complexities of the Israeli-Palestinian conflict.

Periodic attempts at reconciliation between Fatah and Hamas have been made, aiming to establish a united Palestinian front. However, these efforts have been marred by disagreements over governance structures and the overarching approach to the conflict.

The younger generation's growing discontent with the political status quo has fueled grassroots movements and youth activism. The PA must grapple with the evolving aspirations and demands of a demographic eager for change.

Nevertheless, the Palestinian Authority remains a pivotal player in the ongoing Israeli-Palestinian conflict, confronting internal divisions and external pressures. As the region continues to navigate the complex path toward a resolution, the role and effectiveness of the P.A. will undoubtedly shape the trajectory of Palestinian statehood aspirations.

DECODING THE SOLUTIONS: A PATH TO PEACE

*W*ith our understanding of the Israel-Palestinian conflict, we can envisage possible solutions. However, we must also realize that there have been various attempts to resolve this conflict. Therefore, our solution has to consider previous attempts and proposals to allow for a more holistic approach to solving the problem and resolving the conflict.

In this chapter, we will examine the previously proposed solutions and try to chart an onward course from then on.

THE TWO-STATE SOLUTION: NAVIGATING THE PATH TO A SEPARATE PEACE

One of the proposals raised concerning the Israeli-Palestinian conflict is the concept of a two-state solution. This idea envisions the establishment of independent and sovereign states for Israel and Palestine.

The roots of this two-state solution can be traced to the aftermath of World War II. In 1947, with the increasing tensions in the Israel and Palestine region, the United Nations proposed a partition plan. The plan recommended the establishment of separate Jewish and Arab states, with Jerusalem as an international city. As you might remember from the earlier parts of this book, the Jewish leadership accepted the proposal while the Arab leaders vehemently rejected it, setting the stage for the turbulent events that would follow.

Furthermore, the declaration of the State of Israel in 1948 led to immediate conflict. Arab states, refusing to acknowledge the existence of Israel, invaded, sparking the Arab-Israeli War. This conflict resulted in what Palestinians refer to as the Nakba, with hundreds of thousands of Palestinians either fleeing or being expelled from their homes.

The 1960s marked a turning point in the conflict with the establishment of the Palestinian Liberation Organization (PLO). Initially focused on armed resistance, the PLO evolved to advocate for Palestinian self-determination over the years, reflecting a shift in political ideology.

Following the Six-Day War in 1967, Israel occupied the West Bank, East Jerusalem, and the Gaza Strip. The establishment of Israeli settlements in these territories heightened tensions, viewed by Palestinians as obstacles to statehood. The Oslo Accords in the 1990s represented a significant diplomatic effort to achieve a two-state solution. However, challenges such as settlement expansion and disputes over Jerusalem hindered the progress envisioned by the accords.

The conflict went through twists, turns, and milestones as time passed. Recent years have witnessed a notable shift in U.S. policy under the Trump administration. The recognition of Jerusalem as Israel's capital and the relocation of the U.S. embassy were viewed by many as departures from the principles underpinning the two-state solution. The unveiling of the Trump administration's peace plan, often referred to as the "Deal of the Century," raised concerns about the viability of a two-state outcome.

Also, the Abraham Accords, signed in 2020, marked a historic shift in Middle East diplomacy but raised questions about their implications for the Israeli-Palestinian conflict. The accords normalized relations between Israel and several Arab states, illustrating a recalibration of regional alliances. However, the absence of a resolution to the core Israeli-Palestinian issues left the two-state solution's fate uncertain.

Amid these geopolitical shifts, the Israeli-Palestinian conflict has witnessed recurring violence, particularly in the Gaza Strip. The humanitarian impact of these conflicts has been devastating, with civilian casualties and displacement adding to the longstanding challenges faced by the populations on both sides.

As we assess the trajectory of the two-state solution, it is evident that achieving a separate peace remains a formidable challenge. The deep-rooted historical narratives, ongoing geopolitical dynamics, and the complexities of the conflict's human dimension all contribute to the intricate web of challenges.

Though envisioned as a pathway to peace, the two-state solution remains elusive. Its fate is intricately tied to the ever-shifting political landscape, regional dynamics, and the ability of global actors to foster a conducive environment for meaningful negotiations. The journey toward a separate peace for Israel and Palestine continues, marked by uncertainties, but with the hope that a comprehensive and just resolution can be realized in the future.

THE ONE-STATE SOLUTION: PAVING THE WAY TO A UNITED FUTURE

Another one of the proposals for the resolution of the Israeli-Palestinian conflict is the concept of a one-state solution, which envisions a united political entity where Israelis and Palestinians coexist within a shared framework.

This idea of a single, inclusive state in the historic land of Israel and Palestine is not a recent development. It has roots in the early 20th century when discussions about the region's future began gaining prominence. In contrast to the two-state solution, proponents of a one-state vision argue for the creation of a democratic state where both Jewish and Palestinian populations enjoy equal rights and representation.

Advocates for a one-state solution often point to the challenges associated with the two-state model. Issues such as the geographic interweaving of Israeli settlements in the West

Bank, the contested status of Jerusalem, and the complexities of delineating borders have led some to question the feasibility of a two-state arrangement. The ongoing expansion of settlements and the entrenchment of occupation dynamics further complicate the practical implementation of a two-state vision.

Proponents of a one-state solution highlight the shared history, culture, and geography of Israelis and Palestinians. They argue that acknowledging and embracing this shared identity could form the basis for a political framework that transcends ethnic or religious divisions. Such a model, they contend, could foster a sense of unity and collective belonging, overcoming the historical animosities that have fueled the conflict.

The one-state proposal's core is equal rights and representation for all inhabitants, irrespective of their ethnic or religious background. Advocates emphasize the importance of building a political system that safeguards the rights of both Jewish and Palestinian communities, ensuring that neither group is marginalized or discriminated against.

However, while the one-state solution offers an alternative perspective, it has challenges. Critics argue that merging diverse populations with deep-seated historical grievances into a single political entity could exacerbate tensions rather than alleviate them. Questions about the nature of the state, its constitution, and the mechanisms for power-sharing must be addressed to create a system that genuinely promotes coexistence.

Internationally, reactions to the one-state solution vary. Some view it as a pragmatic approach that recognizes the complex reality on the ground. Others argue that it might be a utopian vision, given the deeply entrenched narratives and political realities that have defined the Israeli-Palestinian conflict for decades. Engaging with global stakeholders and garnering international support would be crucial for any proposal seeking to reshape the political landscape.

As we can see, the trajectory of the one-state proposal makes it clear that envisioning a united future for Israelis and Palestinians requires meticulous attention to detail and a commitment to addressing the historical injustices that have shaped their narratives. The road ahead involves navigating complex political, social, and cultural dynamics to build a framework that ensures genuine equality, representation, and peaceful coexistence.

The one-state solution represents a departure from the traditional paradigms of resolving the Israeli-Palestinian conflict. While it introduces novel ideas of shared identity and equal rights, its challenges are substantial. As the discourse on the future of the region continues, the one-state proposal adds a layer of complexity to the ongoing quest for a just and lasting peace in Israel and Palestine.

OTHER PROPOSED SOLUTIONS: NAVIGATING PATHS TO A UNITED FUTURE

In the complex story known as the Israeli-Palestinian conflict, a range of proposed solutions has emerged aside from the two-state and one-state proposals, each reflecting a distinct vision for a united future.

- **Regional Collaborative Initiatives**

One recommended approach involves fostering regional collaborations to address shared challenges and promote stability. Proponents of this approach believe that involving neighboring states in peace-building efforts could create a more comprehensive and sustainable framework for resolving the longstanding dispute.

A historical example illuminating the potential of this approach is the Madrid Conference held in 1991. This event brought together Israel, Palestine, and neighboring Arab states, including Jordan, Lebanon, and Syria, in an unprecedented diplomatic initiative. The conference marked the first time that Israel engaged in direct, face-to-face negotiations with its Arab neighbors.

The Madrid Conference laid the groundwork for subsequent bilateral negotiations, particularly the Oslo Accords between Israel and the Palestine Liberation Organization (PLO). This historic gathering showcased the efficacy of regional collaboration in shaping the political landscape and fostering an environment conducive to diplomatic dialogue.

Proponents of regional collaborative initiatives argue that involving neighboring states brings a broader perspective to the negotiating table. Understanding and addressing the region's shared challenges collectively can contribute to creating a more stable and secure environment for all parties involved.

A regional approach aims to address the immediate issues between Israel and Palestine and the broader dynamics that contribute to regional instability. By fostering cooperation on security, economic development, and cultural exchange, neighboring states can contribute to a comprehensive framework for lasting peace.

While the Madrid Conference represents a historical high point, challenges persist. Geopolitical complexities, historical grievances, and divergent national interests pose hurdles to sustained regional collaboration. However, the potential benefits, including increased security, economic prosperity, and improved diplomatic relations, offer a compelling vision for the future.

As diplomatic efforts evolve, building on the successes of past initiatives becomes crucial. Regional collaborations will provide a platform for dialogue and contribute to a sense of collective responsibility in pursuing peace. The experiences and lessons from the Madrid Conference serve as a valuable resource in shaping future endeavors.

In essence, regional collaborative initiatives stand as a beacon of hope in the turbulent landscape of the Israeli-Palestinian conflict. By fostering understanding, trust, and cooperation among neighboring states, this approach offers a pathway toward a more comprehensive and sustainable resolution that transcends borders and resonates with the shared aspirations of the entire region.

- **Economic Cooperation and Development**

Another proposed avenue for a united future focuses on economic cooperation and development. By fostering joint economic projects, trade initiatives, and infrastructure development, this approach aims to create interdependence, fostering an environment where Israelis and Palestinians have a stake in shared prosperity. However, while this path holds promise, navigating economic collaboration amid political complexities presents challenges.

At its core, economic cooperation seeks to forge connections that transcend political boundaries. Israel and Palestine benefit from shared economic prosperity by engaging in joint ventures and trade agreements. This approach acknowledges the interdependence that economic ties can create, offering a stark contrast to the historical backdrop of political strife.

These joint economic projects can serve as potent confidence-building measures. Collaborative efforts in areas such as energy, technology, and agriculture can create mutual dependencies, fostering an environment where the success of one party is intertwined with the success of the other. This shared stake in prosperity may contribute to a shift in attitudes and perceptions.

Although the economic cooperation proposal holds promise, it also presents its challenges, particularly given the deeply entrenched political complexities of the region. The Israeli-Palestinian conflict is marked by historical grievances, territorial disputes, and geopolitical intricacies that inevitably spill over into economic considerations. Navigating these complexities demands a delicate balance between economic pragmatism and political realities.

Investing in joint infrastructure projects represents a tangible step toward shared development. Whether it's cross-border transportation initiatives, energy grids, or water resource management, these projects have the potential to address common challenges faced by both Israelis and Palestinians. The shared benefits of improved infrastructure can contribute to an atmosphere conducive to dialogue and collaboration. Also, the potential dividends of shared prosperity, improved living standards, and the fostering of mutual dependencies make this avenue a worthy consideration in the quest for a lasting resolution to the Israeli-Palestinian conflict.

- **Grassroots Peace-Building and People-to-People Initiatives**

Grassroots movements and people-to-people initiatives emphasize building connections and understanding among ordinary Israelis and Palestinians. Advocates argue that fostering personal relationships can contribute to a more empathetic and nuanced understanding of each other's narratives. However, the effectiveness of such initiatives is contingent on broader political dynamics and leadership support.

At its heart, grassroots peace-building relies on the premise that meaningful change can arise from the ground up. By encouraging interactions and fostering relationships among individuals from both communities, this approach seeks to break down stereotypes and preconceptions. Face-to-face encounters, whether through cultural exchanges, joint projects, or shared spaces, offer a unique opportunity for people to engage beyond the confines of political rhetoric.

These people-to-people initiatives aim to humanize the "other" by providing a platform for individuals to share their stories and experiences. Through dialogue and shared activities, participants gain insights into the daily lives, aspirations, and struggles of those on the other side of the conflict. This firsthand exposure can challenge ingrained prejudices and contribute to a more nuanced perspective on the multifaceted nature of the conflict.

While grassroots initiatives hold promise, their impact is inevitably shaped by the overarching political landscape. The Israeli-Palestinian conflict is deeply entrenched in historical grievances, territorial disputes, and geopolitical complexities. The success of grassroots movements is contingent on a conducive political environment that allows for the organic growth of understanding and cooperation.

The effectiveness of grassroots peace-building is closely tied to the stance of political leaders and the prevailing political climate. Leadership support can provide the necessary endorsement and resources for such initiatives to thrive. Conversely, political tensions, security concerns, or a lack of political will can stifle the organic growth of grassroots movements.

The international community plays a vital role in supporting and amplifying grassroots efforts. Funding, resources, and diplomatic encouragement from global actors can bolster the impact of people-to-people initiatives. International organizations and NGOs often serve as facilitators, connecting individuals and groups committed to fostering understanding and collaboration.

In essence, this approach represents a valuable avenue for creating lasting change in the Israeli-Palestinian conflict. While their impact may be incremental and not immediately noticeable, the potential for transforming attitudes and fostering a culture of understanding is profound. As individuals from both sides of the conflict engage in dialogue, share experiences, and build connections, they contribute to the larger peace-building effort, promising a more harmonious future in this deeply divided region.

- **Confederation Models**

Some have also proposed a confederation model that allows for distinct national entities while maintaining overarching cooperation in specific areas. This approach seeks to strike a balance between the aspirations of both Israelis and Palestinians for self-determination while acknowledging the need for shared governance in critical domains. However, a workable confederation model involves addressing complex security arrangements and resource management issues.

At the heart of the confederation model is acknowledging two distinct national entities—Israel and Palestine. Rather than pursuing a unified state, the confederation envisions a cooperative framework where each entity retains a degree of autonomy. This cooperative structure accommodates Israelis' and

Palestinians' national aspirations, recognizing their historical narratives and identities.

The essence of the confederation lies in the shared governance of specific domains critical to the well-being of both entities. These domains may include security, water resources, and economic cooperation. By pooling efforts in these areas, the confederation model seeks to foster mutual trust, enhance stability, and address shared challenges that have historically fueled the conflict.

One of the most intricate aspects of the confederation model is the formulation of security arrangements. Given the deeply rooted security concerns on both sides, establishing a system that ensures the safety of Israelis and Palestinians is paramount. The confederation will require a collaborative security apparatus emphasizing intelligence-sharing, joint patrols, and coordinated responses to potential threats. Striking a delicate balance between robust security measures and respecting the sovereignty of each entity poses a significant challenge.

Resource management, particularly in water and economic cooperation, is another focal point of the confederation model. Water scarcity has been a longstanding issue in the region, and a cooperative approach to water resource management is crucial for sustainable development. Similarly, economic collaboration can drive stability, with joint ventures, trade agreements, and shared infrastructure projects contributing to mutual prosperity.

Creating and maintaining a workable confederation model comes with challenges despite the promise of a better coexistence condition. The deeply entrenched mistrust between Israelis and Palestinians, historical grievances, and political sensitivities make the negotiation process exceptionally complex. Issues related to the delineation of borders, Jerusalem's status, and refugees' rights must be navigated with utmost care.

The success of the confederation model hinges on robust international support and effective mediation. The involvement of impartial mediators, possibly under the auspices of international organizations like the United Nations, can provide the necessary oversight and assistance. International actors would play a crucial role in ensuring the implementation of the confederation model and addressing any disputes that may arise.

This confederation model offers a pragmatic path forward in addressing the Israeli-Palestinian conflict. By recognizing the distinct national identities of Israelis and Palestinians while fostering collaboration in critical areas, this approach aims to reconcile competing aspirations. However, the challenges in crafting a viable model should not be underestimated. Diligent international support, sensitive negotiations, and a commitment to shared governance are imperative for the success of the confederation model as a means of achieving lasting peace in the region.

- **Multinational Peacekeeping Forces**

In pursuing stability, multinational peacekeeping forces have been suggested to oversee and enforce agreements between

Israel and Palestine. The presence of an impartial international force aims to provide security assurances for both sides. However, challenges include gaining consensus on the composition and mandate of such forces.

Multinational peacekeeping forces, comprising troops from various countries, are proposed as neutral entities capable of mediating and maintaining peace in regions marred by conflict. In the context of the Israeli-Palestinian conflict, the deployment of such forces aims to create a secure environment, assuaging concerns on both sides and mitigating the risk of escalations.

One of the primary objectives of multinational peacekeeping forces is to offer tangible security assurances. Their presence is designed to instill a sense of safety for both Israelis and Palestinians, fostering an environment conducive to negotiations and the implementation of peace agreements. By acting as a neutral buffer, these forces aim to reduce the likelihood of military confrontations and provide a framework for peaceful coexistence.

While the concept of multinational peacekeeping forces appears promising, the practicalities present significant challenges. Gaining consensus on the composition of such forces involves intricate diplomatic negotiations. Agreement on the countries contributing troops, their rules of engagement, and the scope of their mandate require delicate navigation of geopolitical interests and regional dynamics.

The Israeli-Palestinian conflict is characterized by deeply sensitive territorial and political dynamics. Any proposal involving external forces must carefully consider the sovereignty concerns of both parties. Determining the areas of deployment, access, and the extent of authority granted to peacekeeping forces becomes a nuanced negotiation intertwined with the broader issues at the heart of the conflict.

The deployment of multinational forces also underscores the potential for international mediation. Neutral peacekeeping forces, operating under an international mandate, can mediate disputes, facilitating communication and cooperation between the conflicting parties. The international community's involvement in peacekeeping reflects a collective commitment to resolving the conflict and promoting regional stability.

Implementing multinational peacekeeping forces faces potential political resistance from involved parties. Nationalistic sentiments, historical grievances, and concerns about external interference may hinder the acceptance of foreign troops. Convincing both Israelis and Palestinians of the impartiality and constructive role of peacekeeping forces is a critical aspect of navigating this challenge.

Like most other proposed solutions, the success of multinational peacekeeping efforts hinges on robust international collaboration. Securing funding, resources, and diplomatic support from a broad coalition of nations is essential. International organizations, such as the United Nations, can play a pivotal role in coordinating these efforts and ensuring the sustained commitment of the global community.

This multinational peacekeeping forces proposal presents a complex yet potentially constructive path to addressing the

Israeli-Palestinian conflict. While challenges exist in garnering consensus, navigating territorial sensitivities, and overcoming political resistance, the overarching goal remains the establishment of a secure and stable environment. As international actors explore this avenue, meticulous diplomacy and a comprehensive understanding of the conflict's intricacies will be indispensable to the success of this proposed strategy.

- **Comprehensive Diplomatic Engagement**

Comprehensive diplomatic engagement involves a multifaceted approach to conflict resolution. This includes addressing core issues such as borders, refugees, security, and the status of Jerusalem through sustained negotiations. The Oslo Accords of the 1990s exemplify a diplomatic endeavor that, while facing setbacks, demonstrated the potential for dialogue in shaping the region's future.

This proposed comprehensive diplomatic engagement signifies a commitment to addressing the fundamental components that have perpetuated the Israeli-Palestinian conflict. Rather than focusing on isolated aspects, this approach recognizes the interconnectivity of issues and aims to establish a holistic negotiation framework.

Borders delineating the territories of Israel and a future Palestinian state, the plight of refugees, security arrangements, and the status of Jerusalem stand as pivotal components of this proposal. By engaging in substantive discussions on these matters, diplomats strive to forge agreements that address the root causes of the conflict.

The success of this proposed solution will depend on active international mediation and support. Neutral and impartial third-party facilitators, potentially under the auspices of international organizations, can play a crucial role in guiding negotiations and ensuring adherence to agreements. International actors contribute not only resources but also a broader perspective that transcends the immediate interests of the conflicting parties.

Comprehensive diplomatic engagement offers a vision for lasting peace in the Israeli-Palestinian context. By addressing the core issues systematically, diplomats and negotiators can lay the groundwork for a future where Israelis and Palestinians coexist in security and prosperity. While the challenges are substantial, the potential benefits—regional stability, economic development, and improved relations—underscore the significance of sustained and comprehensive diplomatic efforts.

Each of these proposed solutions has its unique set of challenges. Issues such as political trust, historical grievances, and divergent narratives must be navigated to create a foundation for a united future. The influence of global geopolitics, regional dynamics, and shifts in leadership further complicate the landscape.

Also, engaging with the international community is integral to the success of any proposed solution. Global stakeholders, including major powers, regional actors, and international organizations, are pivotal in providing diplomatic, economic, and security support. Building a consensus among diverse stakeholders remains a significant challenge.

Amid the multitude of proposed solutions, the imperative of inclusive dialogue stands out. Recognizing the diverse perspectives within Israeli and Palestinian societies is essential for any solution to be sustainable. Inclusive dialogues encompassing a broad spectrum of voices, including civil society, women, and youth, can contribute to the framework's legitimacy and durability.

As we navigate the road ahead, exploring alternatives for a united future in Israel and Palestine demands a comprehensive understanding of the historical context, contemporary challenges, and aspirations of the people involved. Crafting a sustainable solution requires innovative thinking, unwavering commitment, and willingness to engage in constructive dialogue that transcends entrenched narratives. The intricate dynamics of the Israeli-Palestinian conflict necessitate a nuanced and adaptable approach, acknowledging the complexity of the issues at hand and working toward a future of coexistence and shared prosperity.

THE ROLE OF THE INTERNATIONAL COMMUNITY: FACILITATING A SOLUTION

The Israeli-Palestinian conflict has consistently drawn the attention of the international community. As a multifaceted and deeply rooted conflict, the involvement of global stakeholders has played a crucial role in shaping diplomatic efforts, peace initiatives, and the pursuit of a just and lasting solution.

Different international organizations, nations, and individuals have been involved directly and indirectly in this conflict at different times. The aftermath of World War II witnessed a transformative period in international diplomacy, marked by the establishment of the United Nations in 1945. The U.N., recognizing the urgency of addressing conflicts and promoting global stability, became a central platform for deliberations on the Israeli-Palestinian question. The pivotal moment came with the U.N. General Assembly's approval of the partition plan in 1947, proposing the creation of separate Jewish and Arab states with Jerusalem as an international city. This resolution laid the groundwork for subsequent developments but faced immediate challenges as Arab states rejected the plan, setting the stage for the Arab-Israeli War in 1948.

The Balfour Declaration of 1917, issued by the British government, expressed support for a "national home for the Jewish people" in Palestine. While serving as a catalyst for increased Jewish immigration, it also contributed to tensions between Jewish and Arab communities. Subsequent U.N. resolutions, particularly Resolution 242 in the aftermath of the Six-Day War in 1967, emphasized the inadmissibility of acquiring territory by force and called for the withdrawal of Israeli armed forces from occupied territories. These legal frameworks continue to shape discussions on the conflict's resolution.

Another involvement of international parties in this conflict is the Oslo Accords. The Oslo Accords, initiated in the early 1990s, represented a significant diplomatic effort with international backing. Facilitated by Norway and endorsed by the United States and Russia, among others, the accords aimed at establishing a framework for resolving the Israeli-Palestinian conflict, including the creation of the Palestinian Authority. While the Oslo process marked a milestone in diplomatic engagement, challenges, including issues related to settlements and the status of Jerusalem, hindered its long-term success.

The Quartet on the Middle East, comprising the United States, the European Union, the United Nations, and Russia, is another instance of international involvement. It emerged as a diplomatic forum to address the conflict. Established in 2002, the Quartet aimed to facilitate the "Road Map for Peace," outlining a series of steps toward a two-state solution. Despite these efforts, the Quartet faced difficulties in ensuring compliance and overcoming fundamental disagreements between the parties.

The United States, as a prominent global power, has played a pivotal role in shaping the trajectory of the conflict. The U.S. has historically been a key ally of Israel, providing diplomatic, economic, and military support. However, navigating a balanced approach that considers the aspirations and rights of both Israelis and Palestinians remains a challenge. Regional actors, including neighboring Arab states, also influence the conflict's dynamics, contributing to the complexity of international involvement.

While international involvement has been integral to diplomatic initiatives, the challenge of achieving consensus among diverse stakeholders persists. Divergent national interests, historical grievances, and geopolitical considerations often impede unified action. Critics argue that inconsistent international pressure, particularly regarding Israel's settlement policies, has hindered the enforcement of resolutions and impeded progress.

The international community also plays a crucial role in addressing the humanitarian consequences of the conflict. Humanitarian assistance, provided through organizations like the United Nations Relief and Works Agency for Palestine Refugees in the Near East (UNRWA), aims to alleviate the suffering of vulnerable populations. However, the persistence of conflict-related challenges, including access restrictions and funding gaps, underscores the limitations of humanitarian efforts without a comprehensive political solution.

As the Israeli-Palestinian conflict persists, renewed diplomatic initiatives and sustained global support remain essential. International actors must navigate the evolving geopolitical landscape, engage with regional stakeholders, and address the core issues fueling the conflict. Building on historical experiences, the international community's commitment to a just and lasting solution can contribute to creating conditions for a peaceful coexistence between Israelis and Palestinians.

The international community's role in facilitating a solution to the Israeli-Palestinian conflict is multifaceted, involving legal frameworks, diplomatic initiatives, global power dynamics, and humanitarian assistance. As the conflict evolves, a comprehensive and coordinated international approach remains crucial for advancing the prospects of a sustainable resolution and a future of peace and stability in the region.

EXAMINING THE WAY FORWARD: AN ONGOING JOURNEY

This seemingly unending conflict between Israel and Palestine continues to defy easy resolution as the region grapples with recurring bouts of violence and political challenges.

As of 2023, the conflict remains characterized by sporadic violence, political impasses, and humanitarian concerns. The recent escalation of tensions, marked by clashes in the West Bank, Gaza, and East Jerusalem, underscores the urgency of finding a sustainable solution. The international community, regional actors, and the parties involved face the complex task of navigating deep-seated issues that have persisted for decades.

The political landscape in both Israel and the Palestinian territories has undergone significant shifts. In Israel, the coalition government led by Prime Minister Benjamin Netanyahu faces internal challenges and external pressures. The coalition's commitment to settlement expansion has raised concerns and added a layer of complexity to peace efforts. On the Palestinian side, internal divisions persist, with Fatah and Hamas holding distinct political and ideological positions.

Diplomatic initiatives remain a key avenue for addressing the conflict. The joint commitment made by Israeli and Palestinian delegates in Aqaba, Jordan, in February 2023 reflects a recognition of the need to curb violence and work towards a just and lasting peace. However, skepticism abounds regarding the feasibility of these commitments, with political leaders expressing reservations, particularly concerning issues like settlement freezes.

The international community's involvement, including the United Nations, the United States, and the European Union, continues to be crucial. Recent statements from the U.K., the U.S., and the E.U. emphasize the commitment to a two-state solution and call for de-escalation. Yet, achieving consensus on the way forward remains challenging, given diverse geopolitical interests and historical alliances.

The humanitarian dimension of the conflict is also a pressing issue. The recent violence has led to casualties and displacement, exacerbating the challenges faced by civilians, particularly in Gaza and the West Bank. Humanitarian organizations, including the U.N. Relief and Works Agency, play a vital role in providing assistance, but sustainable solutions hinge on addressing the root causes of the conflict.

Furthermore, the economic challenges faced by both Israelis and Palestinians contribute to the conflict's perpetuation. Economic disparities, restricted movement, and resource allocation issues hinder the development of viable economies on both sides. Addressing these economic struggles is essential for improving living conditions and fostering an environment conducive to peace.

Education remains a crucial but often overlooked aspect of the conflict. Palestinians and Israelis alike face disruptions to their education due to violence, insecurity, and resource limitations. Nurturing educational opportunities, promoting dialogue in schools, and countering the impact of divisive narratives are vital steps toward fostering mutual understanding and toler-ance among future generations.

The conflict's toll on the region's health infrastructure is another significant issue. Ongoing violence, restrictions on movement, and resource limitations impede access to health-care services. Addressing health challenges requires immediate humanitarian assistance and long-term investments in building resilient health systems that can withstand the pres-sures of protracted conflict.

Examining the way forward for the Israel-Palestine conflict necessitates a comprehensive approach that addresses politi-cal, economic, humanitarian, educational, and health dimen-sions. Sustainable solutions require concerted efforts from the international community, regional actors, and the parties involved. Key considerations include:

1. Political Will and Leadership: Genuine commitment from political leaders on both sides is indispensable. Building trust and engaging in meaningful dialogue are essential to overcoming entrenched positions.
2. International Cooperation: The international community must be committed to facilitating a just and lasting solution. This involves diplomatic engagement, financial support, and sustained efforts to uphold international law and human rights principles.
3. Economic Development: Addressing economic disparities and creating opportunities for prosperity are integral to stability. Inclusive economic policies

can contribute to building trust and fostering cooperation.

4. Humanitarian Assistance: Immediate humanitarian needs must be met, but there should also be a focus on long-term development to break the cycle of dependence on aid.

5. Educational Initiatives: Investing in educational programs promoting tolerance, understanding, and coexistence is crucial for shaping a future generation committed to peace.

6. Health Infrastructure: Strengthening health systems and ensuring access to healthcare for all populations, irrespective of their background, is a fundamental aspect of post-conflict recovery.

In essence, the way forward for the Israel-Palestine conflict is an ongoing journey marked by challenges, opportunities, and the shared responsibility of the international community. While the path may be complex, the imperative to break the cycle of violence, address root causes, and build a foundation for lasting peace remains a shared aspiration that demands collective action.

CONCLUSION

*I*n this comprehensive exploration of the Israeli-Palestinian conflict, we journeyed through the intricate historical, political, and humanitarian dimensions that shape the narrative of this enduring struggle. From the earliest roots in the late 19th century to the contemporary challenges faced by Israelis and Palestinians, the conflict has woven a tapestry of complexities that demand our attention and understanding.

The conflict's roots lie in the competing national aspirations of Jewish and Arab communities during the decline of the Ottoman Empire. The subsequent Balfour Declaration of 1917 and the emergence of Arab nationalism set the stage for the clash of these aspirations. World War II and the Holocaust, while intensifying international support for a Jewish homeland, also fueled Arab resistance.

During the late 19th and early 20th centuries, as the Ottoman Empire waned, nationalist movements gained momentum. In this crucible of shifting powers, the dreams of Jewish and Arab communities collided, setting the stage for a conflict that would define the region for decades to come. The Balfour Declaration in 1917, expressing British support for a "national home for the Jewish people" in Palestine, became a pivotal moment in the trajectory of the conflict.

The post-World War II era witnessed the United Nations proposing a partition plan in 1947, envisioning the creation of separate Jewish and Arab states with Jerusalem as an international city. While the Jewish leadership accepted the plan, Arab leaders vehemently rejected it, setting the stage for further conflict. The declaration of the State of Israel in 1948 led to the Arab-Israeli War, resulting in the mass exodus of hundreds of thousands of Palestinians during what Palestinians refer to as the Nakba, or "Catastrophe."

This period marked the beginning of the Palestinian refugee crisis and set the stage for decades of territorial disputes and geopolitical tensions. Establishing the Palestinian Liberation Organization (PLO) in the 1960s became a defining moment, shifting the Palestinian political landscape towards national liberation and self-determination.

After the Six-Day War in 1967, Israel occupied the West Bank, East Jerusalem, and the Gaza Strip. The establishment of Israeli settlements in these territories further intensified tensions, as Palestinians perceived them as impediments to statehood. The political landscape underwent significant shifts in the 1990s, with the Oslo Accords aimed at a two-state solution. However, challenges such as settlement expansion and disputes over Jerusalem hindered progress.

The persistent cycle of violence, territorial disputes, and the impact of settlements on the ground painted a complex picture of the conflict. The hopes ignited by the Oslo Accords were tempered by the implementation challenges, leading to a reevaluation of the feasibility of a two-state solution.

The Trump era marked a significant shift in American policy and the conflict at large, with the controversial recognition of Jerusalem as Israel's capital. This move heightened tensions, drawing international criticism and reshaping the diplomatic landscape. The Abraham Accords, signed in 2020, presented a novel approach to Middle East diplomacy by normalizing relations between Israel and some Arab nations.

The normalization agreements, brokered by the United States, involved the United Arab Emirates, Bahrain, Sudan, and later, Morocco. These accords represented a departure from the traditional diplomatic stance that linked Arab-Israeli normalization to the resolution of the Israeli-Palestinian conflict. However, they also sparked debates about the potential sidelining of the Palestinian cause in regional discussions.

Recent events have thrust the conflict back into the global spotlight, with recurring violence in the Gaza Strip and political instability within Israel. The clashes, triggered by a myriad of factors, including evictions in East Jerusalem, have led to a significant loss of life and raised urgent humanitarian concerns. The impact on civilians, especially in Gaza, has been severe, with infrastructure destruction and disruptions to essential services exacerbating an already challenging situation. Such a level of violence serves as a stark reminder of the urgent need for a comprehensive and just resolution to the conflict, addressing the grievances of both Israelis and Palestinians.

The proposed solutions, including the Two-State and One-State propositions, alongside alternative pathways, underscore the multifaceted nature of seeking resolution. The international community's role and the ongoing journey toward a solution emphasize the collective responsibility in fostering lasting peace.

The complexities of the Israeli-Palestinian conflict demand an inclusive, informed, and holistic approach to addressing the concerns of both parties. A sustainable resolution requires a commitment to dialogue, understanding, and justice as we navigate the intricate web of historical grievances, geopolitical realities, and humanitarian considerations.

In conclusion, this extended exploration of the Israeli-Palestinian conflict seeks to unveil the heart of a struggle that has endured for over a century. The multifaceted layers of historical, political, and humanitarian dimensions underscore the need for a nuanced understanding of the challenges faced by both Israelis and Palestinians.

The essence lies in recognizing the shared humanity that transcends borders and narratives. A solution to the Israeli-Palestinian conflict demands collective efforts, informed dialogue, and a commitment to justice. By illuminating the multifaceted nature of the struggle, we pave the way for a future where coexistence triumphs over conflict, and the cries for peace resonate louder than the echoes of the past.

I hope that after reading this book you have a better understanding of the Israeli-Palestinian conflict and how they got to where they are now.

LEAVE A 1-CLICK REVIEW

Customer Reviews

☆☆☆☆☆ 2
5.0 out of 5 stars ▾

5 star	▬▬▬▬	100%
4 star		0%
3 star		0%
2 star		0%
1 star		0%

Share your thoughts with other customers

Write a customer review ⬅

See all verified purchase reviews ·

I would be incredibly thankful if you take just
60-seconds to write a brief review on Amazon,
even if it's just a few sentences!

https://amazon.com/review/create-review?asin=1960188224

ABOUT THE AUTHOR

Conrad Presley

Conrad Presley has an academic background in psychology and sociology that uniquely positions him to explore and elucidate the deep-rooted psychological and social factors that underpin this enduring conflict.

Presley has been driven by a relentless quest to understand and explain the psychological undercurrents and social constructs that shape global conflicts. His expertise lies in dissecting complex political narratives and revealing the human emotions and societal pressures that often go unnoticed but play a crucial role in shaping historical events.

In "The Israeli-Palestinian Conflict: Understanding the Forces that Drive Division," Presley applies his scholarly acumen to one of the most intractable conflicts of our time. He meticulously analyzes the historical, cultural, and psychological aspects of the Israeli-Palestinian divide, offering readers a comprehensive understanding that transcends the usual political discourse.

In sum, Conrad Presley is a bridge-builder, connecting the realms of psychology, sociology, and international relations to offer a deeper, more empathetic understanding of global conflicts.

BIBLIOGRAPHY

10 things you should know about the humanitarian situation in Gaza | NRC. (n.d.). Retrieved from https://www.nrc.no/perspectives/2023/10-things-you-should-know-about-the-humanitarian-situation-in-gaza

The 1967 Six-Day War. (n.d.). Retrieved from https://www.wilsoncenter.org/publication/the-1967-six-day-war#:~:text=In%20those%20six%20-days%2C%20Israel,an%20occupier%20and%20regional%20powerhouse

The Abraham Accords - United States Department of State. (2021, January 13). Retrieved from https://www.state.gov/the-abraham-accords

The Abraham Accords, explained. (2023, October 4). Retrieved from https://www.ajc.org/abrahamaccordsexplained

The Abraham Accords: Unlocking sustainable and Inclusive growth across the Middle East | UAE Embassy in Washington, DC. (n.d.). Retrieved from https://www.uae-embassy.org/abraham-accords-sustainable-inclusive-growth

Admin. (2022, December 6). Abraham Accords: Significance | Results | Latest events in 2021. Retrieved from https://byjus.com/current-affairs/abraham-accords

Admin, & Admin. (2020, October 8). The Balfour Declaration and UK recognition of the Palestinian State. . .. - Balfour Project. Retrieved from https://balfourproject.org/the-balfour-declaration-and-the-debate-on-the-recognition-of-the-palestinian-state/

Agencies, M. A. (2015, October 31). Palestinian mourners clash with Israel soldiers at Hebron funerals. *Middle East Eye*. Retrieved from https://www.middleeasteye.net

Amid increasingly dire humanitarian situation in Gaza, Secretary-General tells Security Council Hamas attacks cannot justify collective punishment of Palestinian people | UN Press. (2023, October 24). Retrieved from https://press.un.org/en/2023/sc15462.doc.htm

Arian, A., Shamir, M., & Ventura, R. (1992). Public opinion and political change: Israel and the Intifada. *Comparative Politics*, *24*(3), 317. https://doi.org/10.2307/422135

Ariosto, D. (2023, February 22). The West Bank: a primer. *GZERO Media*.

Retrieved from https://www.gzeromedia.com

Beauchamp, Z. (2018, May 14). Israel-Palestine conflict: The intifadas, explained. *Vox*. Retrieved from https://www.vox.com

Behar, M. (2021, September 23). Were there—and can there Be—Arab Jews? (With afterthoughts on the IHRA definition of antisemitism and Palestinian Jews). Retrieved from https://contendingmodernities.nd.edu/theorizing-modernities/were-there-arab-jews/

Beyer, L. (2023, October 29). How Israel and Palestinians' Troubled History Set Stage For Gaza War. *Bloomberg.com*. Retrieved from https://www.bloomberg.com

Beyond sovereignty and UN recognition: internal challenges to building a resilient Palestinian state. (n.d.). Retrieved from https://odi.org/en/insights/beyond-sovereignty-and-un-recognition-internal-challenges-to-building-a-resilient-palestinian-state

Brodsky, M. R. (n.d.). Trump's Golan decision addresses the limits of Land-for-Peace. Retrieved from https://matthewrjbrodsky.com/22537/trump-golan-decision-addresses-the-limits-of-land

Brym, R. J., & Araj, B. (2023a, November 21). Intifada | History, Meaning, Cause, & Significance. Retrieved from https://www.britannica.com/topic/intifada

Brym, R. J., & Araj, B. (2023b, November 21). Intifada | History, Meaning, Cause, & Significance. Retrieved from https://www.britannica.com/topic/intifada

Chauhan, S., & Chauhan, S. (2023, November 11). Global leaders' understanding of Gaza conflict. Retrieved from https://bnn.network/world/us/contrasting-speeches-shed-light-on-global-leaders-understanding-of-gaza-conflict/

Cohen, R. S. (2017, October 18). Lessons from Israel's Wars in Gaza. Retrieved from https://www.rand.org/pubs/research_briefs/RB9975.html

Consequences of the 1967 war. (n.d.). Retrieved from https://www.washingtoninstitute.org/policy-analysis/consequences-1967-war

Contributors to Wikimedia projects. (2023, April 2). Modern Hebrew. Retrieved from https://simple.wikipedia.org/wiki/Modern_Hebrew

Elections and parties. (n.d.). Retrieved from https://en.idi.org.il/israeli-elections-and-parties/

EP resolutions | Documents | DCAM | Delegations | European Parliament. (n.d.). Retrieved from https://www.europarl.europa.eu/delegations/en/dcam/documents/ep-resolutions

Explainer: UN on the ground amid Israel-Palestine crisis. (n.d.). Retrieved from https://turkiye.un.org/en/249084-explainer-un-ground-amid-israel-palestine-crisis#:~:text=Israeli-Palestinian%20crisis-,The%20United%20-Nations%20has%20been%20working%20in%20the%20Mid-dle%20East,to%20civilians%20on%20the%20ground.

Federman, J. (2023, June 26). Israel OK's plans for thousands of new settlement homes, defying White House calls for restraint | AP News. *AP News*. Retrieved from https://apnews.com

Fenton-Harvey, J. (n.d.). Will the Palestinian Authority survive Israel's war on Gaza? *The New Arab*. Retrieved from https://www.newarab.com

Fieldhouse, D. K. (2008). Palestine: The British Mandate, 1918–1948. In *Oxford University Press eBooks* (pp. 151–219). https://doi.org/10.1093/acprof:oso/9780199540839.003.0005

First intifada. (n.d.). Retrieved from https://www.jewishvirtuallibrary.org/first-intifada

Forey, S. (2023, September 5). Israel's political crisis reaches the Supreme Court. *Le Monde.fr*. Retrieved from https://www.lemonde.fr

Garber, L. (2022, May 12). Internal Palestinian divisions and their consequences. Retrieved from https://www.justsecurity.org/81446/internal-palestinian-divisions-and-their-consequences

Gaza and Israel: The cost of war will be counted in children's lives. (n.d.). Retrieved from https://www.unicef.org/gaza-israel-cost-of-war-counted-children-lives

The Gaza war reverberates across the Middle East. (2023, November 7). Retrieved from https://www.crisisgroup.org/middle-east-north-africa/east-mediterranean-mena/israelpalestine/gaza-war-reverberates-across

Gaza: with each cycle of violence, hearts grow heavier [EN/AR] - occupied Palestinian territory. (2023, June 5). Retrieved from https://reliefweb.int/report/occupied-palestinian-territory/gaza-each-cycle-violence-hearts-grow-heavier-enar

Geneva Solutions. (n.d.). Israel-Gaza conflict: humanitarian law and its defenders shouldn't be collateral victims - Geneva Solutions. Retrieved from https://genevasolutions.news/peace-humanitarian/israel-gaza-conflict-humanitarian-law-and-its-defenders-shouldn-t-be-collateral-victims

Gill, P. S. (2023, October 16). State of War: Israeli-Palestinian crisis and its global ripples. *Nationthailand*. Retrieved from https://www.nationthailand.com

BIBLIOGRAPHY

Ginat, A. (2018). British Mandate for Palestine. *International Encyclopedia of the First World War*. Retrieved from https://encyclopedia.1914-1918-online.net/article/british_mandate_for_palestine

How can educators respond to events in Palestine and Israel? (n.d.). Retrieved from https://www.quaker.org.uk/blog/how-can-educators-respond-to-events-in-palestine-and-israel

The humanitarian health effects of the Israel-Hamas war among civilians in Gaza. (2023, October 20). *Johns Hopkins Bloomberg School of Public Health*. Retrieved from https://publichealth.jhu.edu

Humanitarian Practice Network. (2023, November 21). Responses to the humanitarian situation in Gaza and Israel | Humanitarian Practice Network. Retrieved from https://odihpn.org/publication/responses-to-the-humanitarian-situation-in-gaza-and-israel

The implications of the second intifada on Israeli views of Oslo. (n.d.). Retrieved from https://www.washingtoninstitute.org/policy-analysis/implications-second-intifada-israeli-views-oslo

Iran, the Arabs and Israel: the domino-effect. (n.d.). Retrieved from https://www.opendemocracy.net/en/iran-the-arabs-and-israel-the-domino-effect/

Israel. (2023, October 23). Unmasking the geostrategic chessboard: the Israeli-Palestinian conflict and global powers' hidden agenda. *Medium*. Retrieved from https://medium.com

Israel | Facts, History, Population, & Map. (2023, November 21). Retrieved from https://www.britannica.com/place/Israel/The-second-intifada

The Israel and Gaza war: Economic repercussions | Brookings. (2023, October 24). Retrieved from https://www.brookings.edu/articles/the-israel-and-gaza-war-economic-repercussions/

israel political situation News and latest stories | The Jerusalem Post. (n.d.). Retrieved from https://www.jpost.com/tags/israel-political-situation

Israeli-Palestinian Conflict | Global Conflict Tracker. (n.d.). Retrieved from https://www.cfr.org/global-conflict-tracker/conflict/israeli-palestinian-conflict

The Israel-Palestine Crisis: Causes, Consequences, Portents - occupied Palestinian territory. (2021, May 14). Retrieved from https://reliefweb.int/report/occupied-palestinian-territory/israel-palestine-crisis-causes-consequences-portents

Jazeera, A. (2021, June 8). Israel-Palestine: The politics at play | Start Here. *Al Jazeera*. Retrieved from https://www.aljazeera.com

Jazeera, A. (2023a, June 19). Israel to ramp up settlement expansion in occupied West Bank. *Al Jazeera*. Retrieved from https://www.aljazeera.com

Jazeera, A. (2023b, June 27). Israel approves plans for thousands of illegal settlement homes. *Al Jazeera*. Retrieved from https://www.aljazeera.com

Jazeera, A. (2023c, October 23). What is Hamas? A simple guide to the armed Palestinian group. *Al Jazeera*. Retrieved from https://www.aljazeera.com

Jazeera, A. (2023d, October 25). What has the UN done and said on the Israel-Palestine conflict? *Al Jazeera*. Retrieved from https://www.aljazeera.com

Jazeera, A. (n.d.). Intifada - PalestineRemix. Retrieved from https://remix.aljazeera.com/aje/PalestineRemix/intifada.html

Krauss, J. (2023, October 12). What was Hamas thinking? For over three decades, it has had the same brutal idea of victory | AP News. *AP News*. Retrieved from https://apnews.com

Li, N. (2023, October 11). From 1947 to 2023: Retracing the complex, tragic Israeli-Palestinian conflict. *France 24*. Retrieved from https://www.france24.com

Mahapatra, T. D. (2023, October 11). U.S. must address root causes of Israel-Palestine crisis. *Hindustan Times*. Retrieved from https://www.hindustantimes.com

Master of None: Trump, Jerusalem and the prospects of Israeli-Palestinian peace | Middle East Policy Council. (n.d.). Retrieved from https://mepc.org/journal/master-none-trump-jerusalem-and-prospects-israeli-palestinian-peace

Measuring the impact of attacks on education in Palestine (March 2022) - occupied Palestinian territory. (2022, April 17). Retrieved from https://reliefweb.int/report/occupied-palestinian-territory/measuring-impact-attacks-education-palestine-march-2022

Medina, J. (2019, March 22). What you need to know about the 1987 Intifada | Women, War and Peace | PBS. Retrieved from https://www.pbs.org/wnet/women-war-and-peace/uncategorized/what-you-need-to-know-about-the-1987-intifada/

Meredith, S. (2023, November 2). What is Hamas? What you need to know about the Palestinian militant group that rules the Gaza Strip. *CNBC*. Retrieved from https://www.cnbc.com

Metz, S. (2022, October 17). Israel-Hamas Conflict Locked In by Both Sides'

Strategic Assumptions. *World Politics Review*. Retrieved from https://www. worldpoliticsreview.com

Milestones: 1945–1952 - Office of the Historian. (n.d.). Retrieved from https:// history.state.gov/milestones/1945-1952/arab-israeli-war#:~:text=The%20Arab-Israeli%20War%20of%201948%20broke%20out%20when%20five,Israel%20on%20May%2014%2C%201948

My Jewish Learning. (2021, June 11). Israel's Political Parties. Retrieved from https://www.myjewishlearning.com/article/israels-political-parties/

Nakhoul, S., & Saul, J. (2023, October 10). How Hamas duped Israel as it planned devastating attack. *Reuters*. Retrieved from https://www.reuter s.com

Narea, N., & Zhou, L. (2023, October 10). What is Hamas? Here's what to know about the militant group that controls the Gaza Strip. *Vox*. Retrieved from https://www.vox.com

newsroom. (2023, February 1). Exclusive: Netanyahu says don't get 'hung up' on peace with Palestinians first - thediplomat.gr. Retrieved from https:// thediplomat.gr/exclusive-netanyahu-says-dont-get-hung-up-on-peace-with-palestinians-first/

Nobani, A. (2023, October 29). Palestinians in West Bank face closures, attacks amid Israeli offensive. *Al Jazeera*. Retrieved from https://www.aljazeera.com

Npr. (2023, October 28). Palestinian Authority leader Mahmoud Abbas' role in the Hamas-Israel conflict. *NPR*. Retrieved from https://www.npr.org

The Oslo Accords at 25, the second intifada at 18 | Brookings. (2022, March 9). Retrieved from https://www.brookings.edu/articles/the-oslo-accords-at-25-the-second-intifada-at-18/

Ott, H. (2023, November 15). Israel plans to "destroy Hamas." If that happens, who will lead the Palestinians in Gaza? *CBS News*. Retrieved from https:// www.cbsnews.com

Palestinian political parties & organizations. (n.d.). Retrieved from http://www. mideastweb.org/palestinianparties.htm

Palestinian politics are more divided than ever. (n.d.). Retrieved from https:// www.washingtoninstitute.org/policy-analysis/palestinian-politics-are-more-divided-ever

Peer review of UNRWA's evaluation function. (n.d.). Retrieved from https:// www.kingzollinger.ch/projects-clients/our-projects/project/peer-review-of-unrwas-evaluation-function

Pike, J. (n.d.). Egypt, Israel FMs discuss Gaza ceasefire, Israeli-Palestinian peace process. Retrieved from https://www.globalsecurity.org/military/library/news/2021/05/mil-210531-pdo02.htm

Plan to move UK embassy to Jerusalem raises alarm bells among Palestinians – 10 Mehr – English. (2022, October 5). Retrieved from https://english.10mehr.com/plan-to-move-uk-embassy-to-jerusalem-raises-alarm-bells-among-palestinians/

PLO calls for Britain apology for Balfour. (2016, October 31). Retrieved from https://www.israelnationalnews.com/news/219602

Political and social recomposition in Israel and Palestine. (n.d.). Retrieved from https://www.iemed.org/publication/political-and-social-recomposition-in-israel-and-palestine/

Progressive, Except for Palestine | Opinion | The Harvard Crimson. (n.d.). Retrieved from https://www.thecrimson.com/article/2021/6/24/safi-progressive-except-for-palestine/

Public opinion in the Israeli-Palestinian conflict: From Geneva to disengagement to Kadima and Hamas. (n.d.). Retrieved from https://www.usip.org/publications/2007/06/public-opinion-israeli-palestinian-conflict-geneva-disengagement-kadima-and

Rai, S. K. (2021, March 28). What were the causes and consequences of the 1948 Arab-Israeli war? Retrieved from https://www.e-ir.info/2014/01/15/what-were-the-causes-and-consequences-of-the-1948-arab-israeli-war-2/

Rayman, N. (2014, September 29). Mandatory Palestine: What it was and why it matters. *Time*. Retrieved from https://time.com

Reuters. (2023a, July 14). Israel advances peak number of West Bank settlement plans in 2023, watchdog says. *Reuters*. Retrieved from https://www.reuters.com

Reuters. (2023b, October 12). Israel's parliament approves national unity government. *Reuters*. Retrieved from https://www.reuters.com

Robinson, K. (2023a, March 9). What to know about the Arab citizens of Israel. *Council on Foreign Relations*. Retrieved from https://www.cfr.org

Robinson, K. (2023b, July 12). What is U.S. policy on the Israeli-Palestinian conflict? *Council on Foreign Relations*. Retrieved from https://www.cfr.org

Samuel, S. (2018, March 1). In 1967, Israel's Six-Day War Changed Religion. *The Atlantic*. Retrieved from https://www.theatlantic.com

Second intifada - makan. (2020, October 28). Retrieved from https://www.makan.org.uk/glossary/second_intifada/

Settlement expansion in occupied Palestinian territory violates international law, must cease, many delegates tell Security Council | UN Press. (2023, September 27). Retrieved from https://press.un.org/en/2023/sc15424.doc.htm

Speri, A. (2023, October 14). Before they vowed to annihilate Hamas, Israeli officials considered it an asset. *The Intercept*. Retrieved from https://theintercept.com

Spirlet, T. (2023, October 13). Israel invading Gaza could escalate the war into a larger regional conflict, experts say. *Business Insider Africa*. Retrieved from https://africa.businessinsider.com

Tahhan, Z. A. (2017, October 12). Hamas and Fatah: How are the two groups different? *Al Jazeera*. Retrieved from https://www.aljazeera.com

Tahhan, Z. A. (2018, November 2). More than a century on: The Balfour Declaration explained. *Al Jazeera*. Retrieved from https://www.aljazeera.com

The Editors of Encyclopaedia Britannica. (2023a, October 12). Arab-Israeli wars | History, Conflict, Causes, Summary, & Facts. Retrieved from https://www.britannica.com/event/Arab-Israeli-wars

The Editors of Encyclopaedia Britannica. (2023b, October 26). Balfour Declaration | History & impact. Retrieved from https://www.britannica.com/event/Balfour-Declaration

The Editors of Encyclopaedia Britannica. (2023c, November 18). Palestinian Authority (PA) | Definition, History, & region. Retrieved from https://www.britannica.com/topic/Palestinian-Authority

The Editors of Encyclopaedia Britannica. (n.d.). Six-Day War summary. Retrieved from https://www.britannica.com/summary/Six-Day-War

The General Board of Church and Society. (n.d.). United Nations resolutions on the Israel-Palestine conflict. Retrieved from https://www.umcjustice.org/who-we-are/social-principles-and-resolutions/united-nations-resolutions-on-the-israel-palestine-conflict-6112

Today, A. E. D. U. (2021, May 18). Trauma children in Gaza experience is unlike anywhere else in the world, experts say. *USA TODAY*. Retrieved from https://www.usatoday.com

Today, U. (2023, October 11). Some colleges pull students from study abroad programs in response to Israel-Hamas war. *USA TODAY*. Retrieved from https://www.usatoday.com

U.N. Partition Plan - Project Interchange. (2017, April 20). Retrieved from https://doczz.net/doc/3240517/u.n.-partition-plan---project-interchange

United Nations. (n.d.). Israel-Gaza Crisis | United Nations. Retrieved from https://www.un.org/en/situation-in-occupied-palestine-and-israel

The United States and the Israeli-Palestinian conflict. (n.d.). Retrieved from https://users.ox.ac.uk/~ssfc0005/The%20United%20S-tates%20and%20the%20Israeli-Palestinian%20Conflict.html

U.S. Relations with Palestinian Territories - United States Department of State. (2022, November 25). Retrieved from https://www.state.gov/u-s-relations-with-palestinian-territories/

U.S. Role in the Israeli-Palestinian Conflict. (2006, May 11). Retrieved from https://www.pbs.org/newshour/politics/middle_east-jan-june06-us_05-11

Walk the line: The United States between Israel and the Palestinians | Brookings. (2016, July 29). Retrieved from https://www.brookings.edu/articles/walk-the-line-the-united-states-between-israel-and-the-palestinians/

Washington, A. C., DC. (2021, May 10). Trump and the Israel-Palestine conflict. Retrieved from https://arabcenterdc.org/resource/trump-and-the-israel-palestine-conflict.

What's happening in Gaza? A desperate humanitarian crisis. (n.d.). Retrieved from https://www.redcross.org.uk/stories/disasters-and-emergencies/world/whats-happening-in-gaza-humanitarian-crisis-grows

Wikipedia contributors. (2023a, October 19). Politics of Israel - Wikipedia. Retrieved from https://en.wikipedia.org/wiki/Politics_of_Israel#:~:text=Politics%20in%20Israel%20are%20dominated,revisionist%20Zion-ism%2C%20and%20religious%20Zionism

Wikipedia contributors. (2023b, October 25). List of Jews from the Arab world. Retrieved from https://en.wikipedia.org/wiki/List_of_Jews_from_the_Arab_world

Wikipedia contributors. (2023c, October 27). Palestinian nationalism. Retrieved from https://en.wikipedia.org/wiki/Palestinian_national ism#:~:text=Palestinian%20nationalists%20often%20-drawn%20upon,and%20continue%20to%20do%20so

Wikipedia contributors. (2023d, October 29). Arab Jews. Retrieved from https://en.wikipedia.org/wiki/Arab_Jews

Wikipedia contributors. (2023e, October 29). End of the British mandate for Palestine. Retrieved from https://en.wikipedia.org/wiki/End_of_the_Bri-tish_Mandate_for_Palestine#

Wikipedia contributors. (2023f, November 4). Palestine and the United

Nations. Retrieved from https://en.wikipedia.org/wiki/Palestine_and_the_U
nited_Nations

Wikipedia contributors. (2023g, November 11). Trump peace plan. Retrieved
from https://en.wikipedia.org/wiki/Trump_peace_plan

Wikipedia contributors. (2023h, November 12). First Intifada - Wikipedia.
Retrieved from https://en.wikipedia.org/wiki/First_Intifada

Wikipedia contributors. (2023i, November 12). Palestinian National Authority.
Retrieved from https://en.wikipedia.org/wiki/Palestinian_National_Au
thority

Wikipedia contributors. (2023j, November 14). Balfour Declaration. Retrieved
from https://en.wikipedia.org/wiki/Balfour_Declara
tion#:~:text=The%20Balfour%20Declaration%20was%20a,a%20s-
mall%20minority%20Jewish%20population

Wikipedia contributors. (2023k, November 14). Second intifada - Wikipedia.
Retrieved from https://en.wikipedia.org/wiki/Second_Intifada

Wikipedia contributors. (2023l, November 19). 1948 Arab–Israeli War - Wikipedia. Retrieved from https://en.wikipedia.org/wiki/1948_Arab%E2%80%
93Israeli_War

Wikipedia contributors. (2023m, November 20). Gaza–Israel conflict. Retrieved
from https://en.wikipedia.org/wiki/Gaza%E2%80%93Israel_conflict

Wikipedia contributors. (2023n, November 20). History of the Jews and
Judaism in the land of Israel. Retrieved from https://en.wikipedia.org/wiki/
History_of_the_Jews_and_Judaism_in_the_Land_of_Israel

Wikipedia contributors. (2023o, November 21). Abraham Accords. Retrieved
from https://en.wikipedia.org/wiki/Abraham_Accords

Wikipedia contributors. (2023p, November 21). Fatah–Hamas conflict.
Retrieved from https://en.wikipedia.org/wiki/Fatah%E2%80%93Hamas_
conflict

Yerkes, R. a. T. N. J. B. Y. F. M. H. a. a. H. Z. H. M. M. S. Ü. M. Y. S. (2023, October
13). Arab perspectives on the Middle East crisis. Retrieved from https://
carnegieendowment.org/2023/10/13/arab-perspectives-on-middle-east-
crisis-pub-90774

Yisrael Beiteinu Political Party. (n.d.). Retrieved from https://www.jewishvirtu
allibrary.org/yisrael-beiteinu-political-party

Zeidan, A. (2023, November 21). Abraham Accords | Peace Declaration,
Summary, Countries, & Significance. Retrieved from https://www.britan
nica.com/topic/Abraham-Accords